Defending Europe

The military future of our continent

AUTHORS

Hrvoje Bašić, Ganna Bazilo, Friso Bonga, Laurens Bynens, Katalin Cseh, Benjamin Fievet, Vedrana Gujić, Maximilian Heilmann, Emma Janson, Jorge de Jesus, Lina Karklina, Edgars Lejnieks, William Motsmans, Manel Msalmi, Marcus Nielsen, Aleko Stoyanov, Filip Supel, Anastasia Yasyr, Danica Vihinen (editor).

Cover design: Edgaras Mascinskas

Published by the European Liberal Forum asbl with the support of LYMEC. Co-funded by the European Parliament. Neither the European Parliament nor the European Liberal Forum asbl are responsible for the content of this publication, or for any use that may be made of it. The views expressed herein are those of the authors alone. These views do not necessarily reflect those of the European Parliament, the European Liberal Forum asbl, or LYMEC.

ISBN 978-1-326-87337-0

ELF – European Liberal Forum, asbl
Brussels, Belgium
www.liberalforum.eu

LYMEC – European Liberal Youth, asbl
Brussels, Belgium
www.lymec.eu

Contents

Editor's note by Danica Vihinen, LYMEC secretary general 1

Foreword by Vedrana Gujić, LYMEC president 2014-16....2

HRVOJE BAŠIĆ Defending Europe 3

GANNA BAZILO Implications of the Russian-Ukrainian conflict for the European Security and Defence.................11

FRISO BONGA The Future of European Defence Cooperation...27

LAURENS BYNENS The Benelux Air Defence Pact: a precedent for European Defence cooperation? A Belgian perspective 35

KATALIN CSEH NATO's Strategic Perspective: Rising Challenges in the East...45

BENJAMIN FIEVET Europe needs to step up in response to Russia...52

MAXIMILIAN HEILMANN A European strategy to tackle new methods of war. The European Single Army.............59

EMMA JANSON The Need for European Military Cooperation...67

JORGE DE JESUS European Defence and Security: North Africa and the Sahel 74

LINA KARKLINA Europe's Security: The Role of EU and NATO Between Europe's East and South...........................84

EDGARS LEJNIEKS What Are the Main Threats to the European Security?...90

WILLIAM MOTSMANS The Multi-Speed Approach - A Solution to Europe's Defence Quagmire?...........................96

MANEL MSALMI Towards Cybersecurity: Cyberspace from Fiction to a Real Threat......................................104

MARCUS NILSEN Is the European Union's Mutual Assistance Clause 42.7 a Failure?......................................110

FILIP RAMBOUSEK European Defence Cooperation.......123

ALEKO STOYANOV The Russian Military Challenge to the EU in the Context of the Ukraine Crisis.............................143

FILIP SUPEL Transnational European Military Forces Supporting NATO..159

ANASTASIIA YASYR New Concepts Regarding Security..165

The Authors...171

The Publishers 173

Editor's note by Danica Vihinen, LYMEC secretary general

The essays in this compilation were originally presented at the ELF and LYMEC workshop **"Defending Europe - The military future of our continent"** and the final versions in this compilation draw on discussions during the event. It is worth noting, that the workshop was organised the week before the Brussels attacks in March 2016, and even though the authors were given the possibility to finalise their papers after the event most participants chose to simply include the information and new insights gained during the event, not in the aftermath of the attacks.

During the months that have passed since the event the discussion on a common European defence has gotten more attention and is now a common topic on the agenda in the European institutions. This publication is therefore more timely than ever, and will hopefully provide insight to how young liberals in Europe view the topic.

Foreword by Vedrana Gujić, LYMEC president 2014-16

Once upon a time there was an idea of the EU army. For decades, it was discussed in small groups of idealists and dreamers, always dismissed by EU sceptics, rationalists, strong NATO supporters, and even liberals and pro-Europeans who have been long enough in this topic to become hopeless. After decades of standstill in the field of EU defence, man cannot but become desperate.

But then there came the years of 2015 and 2016 and a line-up of events that changed Europe, its mind-sets, attitudes and behaviours. *Desperate times call for desperate measures.* And rolling out from the back of the cupboard the ideas of European army, Permanent Structured Cooperation (PESCO), increase in defence spending, interoperability, enhanced operational capacities and investments in defence industry, which might eventually lead to the creation of the European Security and Defence Union.

Having all of that in mind and placing the issues of security and defence high on the agenda of the organisation in 2016, LYMEC, with the support of ELF, organised a workshop on the topic of **"Defending Europe - The military future of our continent"**. The event gathered 18 young liberals who researched and analysed the wider range of security related topics, resulting in this compilation of articles.

LYMEC would like to use this opportunity to thank all of the authors for their contributions and for all the time and efforts they've put into this book. We hope this book will contribute to the wider understanding of liberal views on security and feed into the new narrative of European defence.

HRVOJE BAŠIĆ
Defending Europe

Introduction

Current conflicts and crises on the door of the European continent mean that the years of peace in Europe are "past", as we can see numerous threats such as the Russian-Ukrainian crisis, a group of Islamic countries, the complex crisis in North Africa and those could undermine European prosperity.

That situation was extremely serious in 2014. We can see that from the letter of NATO Secretary General Anders Rasmussen, in which he made clear to all members that military budgets are no longer allowed to fall, on the contrary; "Every ally must invest in the necessary resources, which means modern equipment, intensive training of our forces and close cooperation among the NATO allies and with our partners." NATO requires from its members the military budget amounts of 2 percent of GDP, while the average spending on the military budget of member states is between 1.3 percent. A substantial increase in the budget is evident in eastern European countries, Sweden, Latvia, Lithuania, and Estonia - apparently with good reason.

We, the politicians and our media, have to tell our public that decades of peace in Europe after the Cold War, have passed!

In support of this claim we have a document published by the respected think tank European Leadership Network – ELN, members of ELN executive committee are several number of prominent European politicians, former defence minister (e.g. Des Browne from the UK) or Foreign Affairs (e.g. Ana Palacio of Spain) and former NATO Secretary General Javier Solana, and former Russian Foreign Minister Igor Ivanov. "Russia is preparing for conflict with NATO, and NATO is preparing for a possible confrontation with Russia", it's a conclusion according to the study on the topic: "Preparing for the worst: Are the Russian and NATO military exercises making war in Europe more likely?" Therefore, this warning is particularly important.

This conclusion of ELN was emerged by analysing developments after protests in Ukraine last year, when the President Yanukovych had run away from his country. Since then, Russia used that security and administrative vacuum, and they incorporated Crimea. After that, there was a rebellion (strongly encouraged from Moscow) in the provinces of Lugansk and Donetsk in eastern Ukraine. After all, Russia has repeatedly sent their air-force on the NATO airspace border, and launched several large-scale military exercises. Russia has also organized big military exercises with the participation of 80,000 soldiers, 12,000 armoured vehicles, 65 warships, 15 submarines and 220 combat aircraft in March 2015. NATO replied in June with its military exercise. Both operations were primarily aimed at the most vulnerable points in a defensive sense; when it comes to NATO, these are primarily the Baltic states, former members of the USSR which have significant Russian minorities. In the last 20 years Europe had several more crises: the Balkans in the 90's, Georgia in 2008, but with the annexation of Crimea the greatest threat to security and stability in Europe since the Cold War was created.

Today

After the intercept of a Russian aircraft on the Swedish border, the last disturbing report speaks about a Russian simulation-exercise of a nuclear attack on that country! Experts from the "RAND" Corporation believe that, in case of a Russian invasion, the Russian army could have captured the NATO "off guard", and without major problem overran Estonia and Latvia in 36 hours! In fact, all 27 Russian battalions have advanced battle tanks, while 12 NATO battalions does not have any. It ressembles a game of cat and mouse. Besides, the Russian enclave of Kaliningrad, surrounded by NATO countries but armed with numerous missiles, could be another advantage of the Kremlin in relation to the Union.

At this moment, Russia is deploying Army forces in the Arctic, fully prepared for the management of a global war, which can be caused by tensions between world powers. The activity of Russian submarines in the northern part of the Atlantic Ocean is on the level of the Cold War, if not worse! Of even greater concern is not only an increased activity, but also the technological capabilities of Russian submarines which has not been seen before. Russia goes through amazing investments in this area, but the West has no answer to that. Not without reason. It seems that this increase in Russian activity makes European leaders, who can't understand what the Russian strategic and operational objectives are, nervous. Besides the Arctic, Russian activity is also directed towards the Crimea, and to Sakhalin Island in the east, where there is still a dispute with Japan regarding the Kuril islands.

At this moment, Europe is faced with the largest refugee crisis since World War II - hundreds of thousands of refugees have already fled to Europe, while tens of thousands new refugees are waiting for the mercy of the European Community on EU's front door. We are faced with barbed wire at the borders. The "line of defence" has been established – we are defending the Schengen line in Macedonia, by force.

Yesterday we had a united and free Europe without borders - today one divided by wire.

Future

Europe's future will largely depend on the German answer to the refugee crisis, and the other European countries must show more solidarity in order to jointly deal with this historic challenge. No matter the media spoon-feeding, it is undeniable that the situation in Germany is not far from chaos, especially after the New Year's attack in Cologne. Fear is spreading through Germany; buying weapons has significantly increased, demand for pepper-spray has exceeded world demand, and while cities are being patrolled by civil "municipal guards", you can hear gossips about the possibility of a civil war.

Far away from Germany; while we are following the events in Syria, what will happen next in Aleppo could shape the future of Europe.

We could be feeling the consequences for a long time. If the Europeans have learned anything in the last two years, then it would be that we cannot be protected from the consequences of conflicts in the Middle East, nor from the Ukrainian conflict; Russia cannot really be considered as a friend of Europe. Russia's revisionist force is capable of military aggression. In fact, as the fate of unstable Aleppo is holding it's balance, these developments have, like no other since the beginning of this war, highlighted links between the Syrian tragedy and strategic weakening of Europe and the West in general. This balance effect is not only something that Moscow pays their attention to, but Moscow is also directly involved. The spread of instability supports the aim of the Russian dominance. We could say that Putin actually, through the Middle East, wants to expand his influence in Europe, and he received the opportunity for that during the uprising in Ukraine. It is obvious that Putin has used a perfect moment of weakness in the West to stop his hybrid war in Ukraine.

Similarly, the Russian military involvement in Syria has put NATO in a great dilemma, with one of the key members on the front line. While Turkey's relations with Russia are boiling, at the same time Europe desperately urges Ankara to cooperate regarding the handling of refugees. Of course, a new wave of refugees that goes to Europe certainly is in favour of Russia - because the new refugees mean more divisions on the European continent, which strengthens the movement of European right-wingers, who often sympathize with Russia. Aleppo is an open human tragedy. However, it is necessary to connect the dots between the suffering of this city, the European future, and how Russia hangs over both.

Concluding, in order to strengthen the position of Europe in the days ahead, it is necessary to consciously consider our current situation, with all faults, shortcomings and to find solutions, of course. Realistically, NATO has so far functioned "on paper" with the exception of a relatively small conflict in which they participated, but the real question is how it will work in the case of a large-scale conflict?

For example, NATO's actions against ISIL have shown that NATO is alarmingly ineffective. Also, one of NATO's disadvantages is the complicated process of drafting and passing decisions. Namely, in the possible scenario of Russian attacks on Baltic countries, prior to any action on the field, all 28 members of the Alliance should find a consensus with all conclusions, which from the start complicates the situation because there is no quick response. Russia, on the other hand, can implement such a decision in a few hours.

Considering that the European Union is a kind of state with all features (such as currency, parliament, external borders, bank...), my opinion is that EU must strive to the urgent establishment of a joint Union army, following the principles of NATO, but with a more efficient model of action. With this proposal, we are opening the question of establishing our own EU intelligence network/agency. Absurdly, the NATO Alliance does not have its own intelligence network.

Finally, let us not forget; our Europe has produced the two bloodiest wars in human history, and if we want to preserve Europe as we built it after World War II, Europe as a symbol of democracy and dialogue, Europe as the capital of human rights - we must take new powerful steps which will ensure peace and stability on our continent. As liberals, we must always strive primarily for dialogue and agreement, but we must also be prepared of self-defence and the necessary use of force, as a last line of resistance!

GANNA BAZILO
Implications of the Russian-Ukrainian conflict for the European Security and Defence

Introduction

Events, which took place in Ukraine two years ago, completely changed not only the future of this country, but greatly influenced security and defence structures in Europe. With the illegal annexation of Crimea by the Russian Federation and the outbreak of a military conflict in Eastern Ukraine, the European continent has experienced several security shocks. First, the borders of a sovereign European state were illegally modified for the first time since the end of the Second World War. Secondly, this situation shocked the established international legal order since Russia violated fundamental international, regional and bilateral charters and treaties, establishing peace and security in Europe.

Thirdly, European security space is not targeted purely by military means, but by a complex of alternative measures which reach through the border-protected areas into a daily life of Europeans. The so-called 'hybrid warfare' – a concept described by the NATO as a "blend of conventional/unconventional, regular/irregular, and information and cyber warfare"[1] - waged by Russian against Ukraine and Europe in the form of economic blockade, trade bans, cuts of gas supply and transit as well as disinformation campaigns, also finds its elements in multiple Russian-speaking communities in the EU countries.

What does this situation mean for Europe and its citizens and how should Europe react to this challenge? Is there only a political solution to this crisis or should there be a stronger approach? This paper would like to identify to what extent the Russian-Ukrainian military conflict influences the military future of the European continent in order to answer to these questions.

The first part of this paper will examine current state of the conflict in Ukraine, outcomes of the implementation of the Minsk agreement and diplomatic efforts to its resolution. The second part will look at the way key international political and security actors (the UN, the NATO and the EU) responded to this crisis. The final part will analyse the efficiency of these responses and elaborate on the

---

[1] Dr. Damien Van Puyvelde, *"Hybrid War - Does It Even Exist?"*, 2015, NATO Review: http://www.nato.int/docu/Review/2015/Also-in-2015/hybrid-modern-future-warfare-russia-ukraine/EN/index.htm

impact of the Ukrainian crisis on European security and defence strategy.

Part I: Minsk peaceful process: is it a way out?

The Minsk II agreement was reached in the Belarussian capital on 12 February 2015 following a dramatic escalation of military activity in Eastern Ukraine. Its 13 points provided for a roadmap to de-escalation of the conflict and its further resolution with first steps to be full ceasefire and withdrawal of heavy weapons from the front line.[2] Other immediate provisions would include release of hostages, reestablishment of control over the Ukrainian-Russian border and a launch of a dialogue on the local-elections and special regime for the occupied territories.

The deadline which was set up for the end of 2015 has passed and as of March 2016, the situation still remains far away from full implementation of at least a single point:

- the ceasefire is breached on a daily basis with the tendencies to increased shelling by separatist towards mid-March 2016;[3]

---

[2] BBC, Ukraine ceasefire: New Minsk Agreement key points, 12 February 2015, http://www.bbc.com/news/world-europe-31436513
[3] Daily reports of the HQ of the anti-terrorist operation, source: http://uacrisis.org/stream

- the withdrawal of heavy weapons is not completed, instead the OSCE SMM reports "the use of restricted weapons across the line of contact"; [4]

- representatives of the OSCE Special Monitoring Mission (SMM) for a long time did not have access to the non-government controlled areas of Donetsk and Luhansk oblast, however the situation is reported to be improved;[5]

- the Russian-Ukrainian border remains under control of pro-Russian separatists;

- Over 137 Ukrainian hostages remain kept by Russian and so-called authorities of DNR and LNR[6], including some high level political prisoners like Nadiya Savchenko (still under trial), Oleg Sentsov and Oleksander Kolchenko (sentenced to 20 and 10 years in Russian colonies).

---

[4] OSCE SMM report from 26 February 2016: http://www.osce.org/ukraine-smm/224211?download=true

[5] Latest from the OSCE SMM to Ukraine, based on information received as of 19:30, 9 March 2016: http://www.osce.org/ukraine-smm/226846

[6] As of 16 February 2016, http://politic.kiev.ua/regions-suspilstvo/13861geraszenko-nazvala-kilkist-ukrainskih-viiskovopolonenih.html

14

Both sides blame each other for the violations of the agreement. While Ukrainian side puts responsibility for daily shelling on separatists and supply of weapons on Russia, the other side points out on the non-implementation of the political provisions which envisage amnesty and legally determined special status for Donetsk and Luhansk regions in the Ukrainian Constitution (Annex 1).

On 31 August 2016, the Verkhovna Rada of Ukraine adopted in the first reading changes to the Constitution of Ukraine in the part of decentralization – an action, which provoked public protests and cost lives of four servicemen ensuring order at the doors of the Parliament. Furthermore, it is with the vote for this draft, when one could trace the beginning of a current political crisis and a break inside the pro-European coalition (exit from the coalition of the Radical Party and no-vote by the Batkivschyna Party). As of today, there are not enough of the required 300 votes in the chamber to go through the adoption in the second reading of the constitutional amendments on decentralization. Moreover, subjects of a special status for Donbas and amnesty - are rather negatively perceived by the majority of the Ukrainians.[7]

---

[7] Sociological Survey "Social and Political Sentiments of Ukrainians (Section 2: War and Peace)", Gorshenin Institute, 1 March 2016:

At the same time, the Minsk negotiation process receives not only negative assessment. Politicians involved and experts acknowledge that it helped preventing further escalation in the East and "contributed to a sharp decline in causalities" which, according to the UNCHR report amounts for over 9 000 people lives since the beginning of the conflict.[8] Secondly, since the last big battle of Debaltseve in February 2015, there were no major shifts of the front line between the government and non-government controlled areas. Thirdly, the second protocol of the Minsk agreement has foreseen an important provision on humanitarian assistance access to the separatist-controlled areas. As a result of negotiations, the International Red Cross was allowed to provide humanitarian assistance to around 2,5 million people remain living on the occupied areas. Additionally, measures were taken for the people living in so-called "grey zones" along the contact line (up to 1 million persons). Finally, the negotiations in the Minsk format helped the overall stabilisation of the situation in the East to the extent that some displaced people decided

---

http://gorshenin.eu/news/224_social_and_political_sentiments_of.html
[8]   http://www.theguardian.com/world/2015/dec/09/ukraine-conflict-9000-dead-says-un

to return to their homes and the process began to de-mine the affected territories.[9]

Both the Normandy format talks and the Minsk Trilateral Contact Group (TCG) keep their meetings and the deadline for the implementation of the Minsk provisions was extended into 2016 with little progress coming out from them so far.[10] However, as Ms. Geraschenko, Special Representative of the President to the TCG puts it: "The agreement is not implemented, but it is working"[11] – first and foremost because it is directly linked with the economic sanctions imposed by the EU on the Russian Federation. Therefore, the next part will look into the measures taken by the key

---

[9] Interview of Iryna Geraschenko, Member of Parliament, Special Envoy of the President to the Minsk Trilateral Contact Group, 5 Channel, Ukraine, 8 January 2016: http://www.5.ua/interview/Iryna-Herashchenko-Minski-uhody-ne-vykonuiutsia-ale-pratsiuiut--inakshe-ne-bulo-b-sanktsii-proty-Rosii-102881.html

[10] UNIAN: Hard Talks in Paris: statements of Normandy Quartet MFs: http://www.unian.info/politics/1282625-hard-talks-in-paris-statements-of-normandy-quartet-fms.html

[11] Interview by Iryna Geraschenko, Member of Parliament, Special Envoy of the President to the Minsk Trilateral Contact Group, 5 Channel, Ukraine, 8 January 2016: http://www.5.ua/interview/Iryna-Herashchenko-Minski-uhody-ne-vykonuiutsia-ale-pratsiuiut--inakshe-ne-bulo-b-sanktsii-proty-Rosii-102881.html

international actors in order to solve the crisis in Ukraine.

Part II: International responses to the Ukrainian crisis

When peaceful protests in support of the EU Association began in Kyiv, nobody expected it to escalate to the extent of illegal annexation of Crimea and the open military conflict in the East with thousands dead and millions displaced. Therefore, the reactions and responses took some time to be formulated. By illegal annexation of Crimea, Russia violated the fundamental texts of the United Nations, statues of the Council of Europe, the Final Helsinki Act (1975) and the Budapest Memorandum (1994) and several bilateral treaties signed with Ukraine.[12] The logical step would be to expect strong reaction from the guarantors of international legal order and security.

The Permanent Representation of Ukraine to **the UN** called the first Security Council meeting on 28 February 2014, but it was not until 27 March 2014 when the General Assembly adopted a Resolution on

---

[12] Jean-Dominique GUILIANI, "Russia, Ukraine and International Law", Policy Paper, Robert Schuman Foundation, European Issues, No 344, 17 February 2015.

the Territorial Integrity of Ukraine.[13] Taking into account that Russia, as a permanent member of the UN Security Council with the veto right, is not accepting its responsibility neither for Crimea, nor for Donbas, diplomatic fights in the premises of the UN, are still on-going in parallel with the real battles in Eastern Ukraine. However, with the election of Ukraine as a non-permanent member of the UNSC for 2016 - 2017 there is a hope that Ukrainian diplomats will be able to introduce necessary procedures and mechanisms allowing for more justice for Ukraine in this conflict.

Another immediate appeal of Ukraine was to **the NATO** as a key organisation ensuring military defence for European states. Almost all members of the EU are also NATO members and therefore, in case of external military aggression are protected by the Article 5 of its Statute. On papers, Ukraine has been long time aspiring to become a member of this military organisation. However, when Yanukovic was elected President in 2010, one of his first steps was to discharge completely the Center on Euro-Atlantic Integration and the Commission on the preparation for Ukraine's membership in this organisation. Therefore, for years Ukraine's participation in the NATO structures remained at the level of "distinctive

---

[13] United Nations, The Situation in Ukraine: Quick Guide, http://research.un.org/en/ukraine

partnership", with the country having participated in military trainings and sending its soldiers to the NATO-led operations.

Following the annexation of Crimea and the military outbreak in the East, NATO members "condemned Russia's military action against Ukraine" and "suspend all practical civilian and military cooperation with Russia", leaving the political contacts "at the level of ambassadors and above"[14]. The NATO Summit in September 2014 "pledged to support the efforts of the Ukrainian government to pursue a political path" and agreed on "a comprehensive and tailored packaged of measures to help Ukraine better provide for its security"[15]. Hence, they reinforced previously established areas of cooperation with Ukraine and set up Trust Funds which would allow the NATO members and its partners to voluntary contribute to the capacity-building programs for Ukraine in 5 areas: 1) command, control, communications and computers; 2) logistics and standardisation; 3) cyber defence; 4) military career transition; 5) medical rehabilitation. While assisting Ukraine with strengthening its military

---

[14] NATO, Responses to the Ukraine - Russia conflict:
http://www.nato.int/cps/en/natolive/topics_37750.htm
[15] NATO website:
http://www.nato.int/cps/en/natolive/topics_37750.htm

capacities, NATO did not provide any defensive weapons or sends its troops to fight in Eastern Ukraine.

The first reaction of **the European Union** to the illegal annexation of Crimea was an introduction of "travel bans and assets freezes against persons involved in actions against Ukraine's territorial integrity".[16] On 13 March 2014 the European Parliament adopted a very strong *Resolution on the Invasion of Ukraine by Russia* using strong language condemning Russian action.[17] Later in July 2014, the EU imposed economic sanctions, linked to the tragic downing of the flight MH17. A year later, in March 2015 the restrictive measures were linked by the Council to the complete implementation of the Minsk agreements, therefore, most recently they were once again extended until September 2016. The EU and Member States refrain from any military assistance to Ukraine. Its leadership promotes "only political and diplomatic solution" to this crisis by the fulfilment of the Minsk agreements. Jointly with the EU, sanctions against Russia were also introduced by the US, Canada, Australia, Norway, Switzerland and Japan.

According to numerous reports and assessments, these economic sanctions, doubled with the

[16] http://europa.eu/newsroom/highlights/special-coverage/eu_sanctions/index_en.htm

[17] http://www.europarl.europa.eu/sides/getDoc.do?pubRef=-//EP//TEXT+TA+P7-TA-2014-0248+0+DOC+XML+V0//EN

tremendous fall in oil prices, are so far the most effective measure taken by the international community against Russia which indirectly affected Russia's behaviour in Eastern Ukraine. Thus, researches observe that in the course of the conflict Russia has modified its tactics towards Ukraine. First, taking up on the independence claims of separatists, they wanted to "to establish a pro-Russian "Novorossia" enclave", but when this idea did not work, the goal is "to 'implant' in Ukraine the occupied territories in their current form and on Russian terms".[18] While the question of Crimes is still a red rug to be raised at the negotiations, with every day it becomes more and more costly to support the annexed Crimea with the recent trade and energy blockade imposed by the Ukrainian government as a result of active lobby of the Crimean Tatars.

Part III: Impact of the Ukrainian crisis on European security and defence strategy

While military and defence policies belong to the competences of the Member States, there is now a growing understanding that first, no single state can face the security challenges alone and second, that in

---

[18] *"Ukraine-Russia Relations: From "Strategic Partnership" to Coexistence"*, Razumkov Center article, The Russian-Ukrainian Conflict: Current State, Implications, Scenarios, Razumkov Center Library, Kyiv, 2015, p. 10.

the current international setting there is a need to strengthen EU's defence in complementarity to NATO. The idea for a common defence policy is not a completely new, however it is with the increasing instability in the EU's immediate neighbourhood and constantly developing unconventional attacks that there is an obvious need for a stronger European response not only in normative, but also in military terms.

EU leaders openly state that what happened in Ukraine is an attack against the European security. Russian aggression in Ukraine has completely transformed the Black Sea region military landscape. Only in one year after the annexation the defensive force which existed in Crimea has been transformed into a strike force for Russia including with nuclear weapons (Annex 2). With this strategic position in the Black Sea, well-functioning military fleet and stolen Ukrainian military basis, Russia could easily threaten European countries in Central Europe, the Balkans, Southern Europe and also Eastern Mediterranean and even the Middle East.[19] Moreover, Russia could apply the same logic of "protecting Russian-speakers abroad" as a justification for intervention into the Baltic States which have large Russian communities remaining from the Soviet Union

---

[19] EP Press Release, Russia has transformed Black Sea military landscape, say foreign affairs MEPs, 5 May 2015.

times. Furthermore, many times waters and airspace of the Baltic and Nordic states were violated by Russian military.

The European Agenda on Security presented in 2015 aims at setting a coordinated response for security challenges and outlines three key priorities for the European security: strong response to terrorism and foreign terrorist fighters, organised cross-border crime and cybercrime. It was also agreed to reinforce the NATO-EU relations and as the Secretary General Stoltenberg puts it: "NATO is implementing the biggest increase in our collective defence since the end of the Cold War".[20] Instead of cutting funds for defence, it was agreed to increase spending to at least 2% of GDP over the next decade.

However, what is lacking is the reinforcement of the EU's Common Security and Defence Policy (CSDP) which is operating peace-keeping operations and conflict prevention mission. More autonomous operations abroad could contribute greatly to the stabilisation of the neighbourhood and tackling the

---

[20] Remarks by NATO Secretary General Jens Stoltenberg at the European Parliament Committee on Foreign Affairs, 23 February 2016:
http://www.nato.int/cps/en/natohq/opinions_128311.htm?selectedLocale=en

new hybrid challenges facing the European continent.[21] The strengthened CSDP would not mean complete militarisation of the European project, but a complimentary pillar of its normative power and its actions in foreign, security and development policies.

Conclusions

Targeted military aggression by Russia in Ukraine since 2014 has changed the security architecture in Europe and severely damaged international legal order. Not only it caused death of thousands and millions displaced Ukrainians, it has scaled up more dangerous and often invisible 'hybrid' threats to Europeans. While it seems like there is no imminent invasion threat for the EU Member States for the moment, Russia's foreign policy is unpredictable in its actions and does not fall into any internationally excepted standards.

While the Minsk peace process aimed at solving military conflict in Eastern Ukraine has a slight hope of being implemented, the question of Crimea's return to Ukraine is not included neither in the Minsk agreement, nor linked to the sanctions imposed by the EU against Russia. In fact, Russia used all possible means to turn the peninsular into its military base within the two years of occupation. Taking into

---

[21] ALDE Roadmap towards EU Integrated Military Forces, 2015.

account Crimea's strategic geographical location, there is now a much closer access for Russia to strike European countries in Central and Eastern Europe.

Therefore, the next years will be crucial for European security and defence policy. The EU Members States can rely on the NATO for its defence and there are concrete actions taken for strengthening the EU-NATO cooperation. However, there is a common understanding that there is a need for enhancing Europe's common defence mechanisms and responses to security threats inside and outside its borders, including the development and more autonomy to the CSDP and unlocking its full potential to provide security and stabilization in Europe's neighbourhood.

Annexes:

Infographics: One year after Minsk Agreement
http://uacrisis.org/wp-content/uploads/2016/02/Minski-ugodi-ENG.jpg

Infographics: Militarized nuclear Crimea is a threat to Europe and the world: http://uacrisis.org/20272-militarized-nuclear-crimea-threat-europe-world

FRISO BONGA
The Future of European Defence Cooperation

The European Commission and a variety of European political parties have spoken out in favour further integration of European defence capabilities and the eventual creation of a European army. Also within NATO the non-European partners are urging the EU to increase their capacity and take more responsibility for European security.

Within the European Liberal Youth the subject has proven controversial however. Although it seems only logical that a Common Security and Defence Policy can only be supported by a Common European military force - there is no denying the significant challenges. In this essay, I will outline the main arguments, discuss the challenges that need to be dealt with and offer a way forward.

Discussion on the cooperation and possible integration of European armed forces revolves primarily around three distinct themes. These themes all have their merit, but they carry different weight. They will be treated below in an ascending order: first the cultural objections, then military necessity and finally the major political question of democratic sovereignty.

Many of the objections to a European army, although presented as practical, are of a cultural nature. The language barrier is an often-heard example of this. Another argument focuses more on the differences in military identity or doctrine between different EU countries.

Both arguments are based on the traditional notion that European countries have fundamentally different characters: Northern Europeans are rigid, Southern Europeans are lazy, and so on. All of them, always and everywhere. Out-dated as this may seem after decades of EU cooperation, the classical east-west and north-south divides have prevailed and have a tendency to manifest themselves especially during crises.

Therefore, it has proven unwise to discard such prejudice as emotional remnants of a feudal Europe. On the contrary, if its differences can be addressed, European diversity would be a source of versatility and strength for future, European, armed forces.

The complete integration of European armies is still far away, but there is a lot of cooperation between EU member states already. NATO's Rapid Deployment Force and the EU Battlegroups are multilateral examples this, although they do illustrate ineffectiveness and shortcomings more than anything else.

The most far-reaching example of integration is the German-Dutch Declaration of Intent from 2013, and subsequent integration of the Dutch Air Assault Brigade into the German Division Schnelle Krafte.

This example shows, as has been argued by CSIS's Stefan Soesanto, that an integration of forces can actually increase national sovereignty and does not detract from it.[22] At the same time, the Dutch-German initiative shows the advantages and potential of regional cooperation, as opposed to the continental cooperation in the EU Battlegroups.

From a military perspective, the arguments regarding cooperation leading to integration are mainly positive. If we look at the question through military glasses the answer is simple: military integration is the only way in which the EU can keep up with worldwide military development and provide its member states with the sort of independence it needs to guard European interests.

Whether it is to protect borders and territory, to provide stable and safe area's in neighbouring regions or to quickly and decisively act when international law is threatened or crimes against humanity are

---

[22] S. Soesanto, 'Europe needs less soldiers – but more European ones', http://www.nato.int/docu/review/2015/Also-in-2015/europe-defence-budget-military-soldiers/EN/index.htm

perpetrated in our backyard. This level of ambition has been evident since the treaty of Amsterdam stipulated the Petersberg Tasks, but the EU still lacks the means to effectively pursue it.[23] For an illustration of the level of ambition, see the map below:

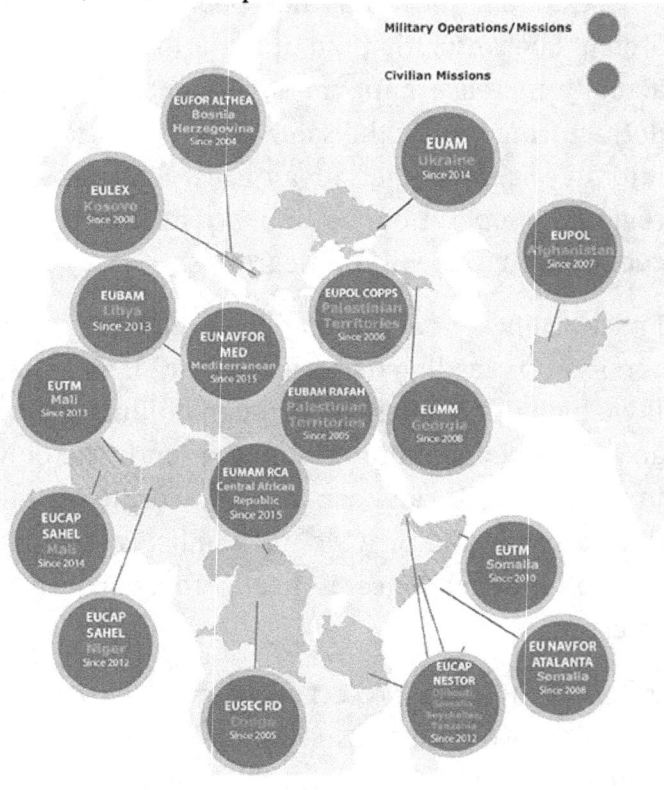

---

[23] European External Action Service, 'Ongoing Missions and Operations', http://www.eeas.europa.eu/csdp/missions-and-operations/; European External Action Service, 'Military Headline Goals', http://www.eeas.europa.eu/csdp/about-csdp/military_headline_goals/index_en.htm

(Map source: http://www.eeas.europa.eu/csdp/missions-and-operations/)

The most important institutional European contribution to continental defence cooperation is the European Defence Agency. Since its foundation this organisation has been working on the coordination of national defence planning. Right now, this is a more crucial step in the process of defence integration than the actual integration of operational units. It is crucial for two reasons. First of all, pooling as much of the 28 fragmented defence budgets into joint programs is an important step towards increasing the efficiency of European defence spending. The current situation proves that you can't spend the same Euro twice, but that you can spend 28 different Euro's on the same thing. The wastefulness and inefficiency of this should keep more people awake. Secondly, coordination of defence planning encourages member states to work together and decide on common defence goals. In doing so the work of the EDA strengthens the alignment of the different military doctrines and exponentially increases the interoperability of European armed forces. Without much attention so far, the EDA has been working towards increased cooperation in areas where financial capacity has more weight than troop numbers, areas where the huge economic potential of the Union can be leveraged to exponentially increase military capacity.

Currently the EDA is working on a variety of programs, in the fields of satellite communications, R&D and airlift capacity. Yet despite its important contributions to EU security political resistance hinders the work of the EDA. The opposition is led by Great Britain, that has constantly blocked any increase or in correction for inflation of EDA budget. This is as much a cultural problem as it is a political one.

This opposition comes from a fear that a strong and integrated EU military component would jeopardize the 'Special Relationship' between the UK and US. Which, in turn, is interpreted as detrimental to British capabilities to guard its interests. This is an argument heard in many European capitals and it brings us to the main challenge in the political spectrum: national sovereignty and the fundamental authority of national parliaments when it comes to matters of defence.

In the current political reality, only national representative bodies can decide on the defence of national territory or situations where military personnel are to be sent in harms way. From a point of democratic oversight and accountability this is a fundamental right of the national parliaments. Over the last six decades, all member states have developed this right in their own way. Consequently, every European country has its own procedure for deciding on war or peace. In the process of defence cooperation this poses a problem. Should two, three, of worse, 28 member states decide on a joint military operation, the parliamentary processes to approve it, turn to a swampy maze of different rules, demands and timelines. In the case of a NATO article 5 event, there are procedures to overcome this. Yet such work-arounds are unavailable outside NATO conditions - such as a hypothetical case where the EU would want to act quickly on the threat of genocide in a neighbouring region. The result is too often an understandable reluctance to decide on joint military operations, or, in cases where such a decision is taken, to disappointment leading to distrust.

While the national sovereignty on military action is legitimate and necessary until a valid democratic alternative is available supranationally, there is no stringent reason why the procedures shouldn't be better coordinated. In order to make significant progress on the integration of European defence capabilities, increasing parliamentary cooperation and harmonization of procedures is by far most important step. The difficulty of this should not be underestimated, but neither should its importance. It should be noted that the goal is not standardization. Every nation has its own interests and history to take into account. But the process of exchanging information, best-practices and time frames in the search of common ground, will strengthen mutual understanding and bring the national parliaments closer together on military issues. This is not to say that political differences will cease to exist, but the forum and terms on which they will be discussed can, and should, be more pan-European.

To conclude, there are three ways in which European defence cooperation should move forward. First of these is the harmonization of the different parliamentary procedures regarding national defence and military deployment. Second, regional cooperation should be increased. The step towards a joint European force - with all nationalities into a single unit - is at this point unrealistic and for the near future undesirable. Regional cooperation on the other hand, offers great potential to begin to overcome differences in culture, language and interests. The third step forward is increasing the scope and funding of the EDA, so that the 28 defence budgets can be spent more efficiently and increase interoperability between European military forces.

If these steps are taken carefully and deliberately, they will drastically increase European military capability and, consequently, strengthen Europe's ability to guard its interests and protect its values.

LAURENS BYNENS
The Benelux Air Defence Pact:
a precedent for European Defence
cooperation? A Belgian perspective

The Benelux Air Defence Pact

On March 4 2015, the Netherlands, Belgium and Luxemburg signed an agreement on the joint air policing of their territories. This includes both the protection of their air spaces and the sharing of intelligence in this domain. In 2004, Belgium took the initiative by sending an invitation to Luxemburg, France, Germany and the Netherlands to work together on renegades[24]. In 2013, the Benelux countries signed a letter of intent. From 2017 onwards, Belgian and Dutch fighter jets will protect the Benelux air space. Luxemburg has no fighter jets, but it opens

---

[24] In 2015, the Belgian parliament approved a bilateral agreement with France on renegades. If a renegade were to fly above Belgium into France, normally Belgian pilots would have to stop at the French border. But because of the agreement they can follow the renegade into France. This way, the renegade can be followed closely in order to gather more information (type of airplane, flight route, etc.), but the fighter jet cannot use lethal violence. Germany and Belgium are working on an agreement. The details of this agreement are not yet known. (Belgische Kamer van Volksvertegenwoordigers, 2015a; 2015b).

its air space to its neighbours' jets and pays its part of the burden. The March meeting took place in the Netherlands, at which many members of the Belgian government were present. This was seen as a strong signal that Belgium takes this agreement very seriously.

Under the agreement, the Netherlands and Belgium will take turns to guard the airspace of the entire Benelux. This means when for example Dutch fighter jets are on duty, the Belgian government might have to instruct Dutch pilots to use lethal violence against a hostile target that has entered the Belgian airspace. The Benelux Air Defence Pact is concerned with two kinds of situations: on the one hand, in case of a Quick Reaction Alert (QRA). On the other hand, in case of a renegade.

The agreement lays down strict rules concerning which actions are allowed and which political authorities must be involved in the decision. It should bring down the costs of air defence for all the Benelux countries because of the pooling and sharing of capabilities. The Belgian government has indicated that the Benelux agreement "has as its goal to improve the intervention capabilities of the parties involved with regard to renegades through a synergy of efforts and by the pooling and sharing of resources [translated from Dutch]" (Belgische Kamer van Volksvertegenwoordigers, 2016a: 3).

Quick Reaction Alert

The first area of cooperation under the Benelux Pact concerns QRA. Whenever an unidentified airplane (e.g. a fighter plane, a bomber) enters a country's airspace, the air force is warned to stand ready. Often, NATO's air command has already notified the national air force. If NATO gives the order to scramble, fighter jets are on their way within minutes to meet the potential threat in case it should enter the country's airspace. If all goes well, the fighter jets are able to contact the other airplane and escort it out of the country's airspace.

The pilots have number of options to make clear that the airplane must change its course: they can for example examine the target through visual or electronic identification, or they can fire warning shots with flares or with ammunition.

The coordination is thus done by NATO, who cooperate with the national defence authorities. The analysis of the situation takes place at a Combined Air Operations Centre (CAOC). Ultimately, if concrete military actions are needed, the country where the situation is taking place takes the final decision. This line of procedure is the same in all NATO member countries. When the target leaves the national airspace and flies into the airspace of another NATO country, the latter's fighter jets have already been briefed and are ready to take over at the border (Defensie.nl; Belgische Kamer van Volksvertegenwoordigers, 2015a: 18).

Renegade

The second kind of common mission is aimed at the collective identification and possible actions against a so called 'renegade'. It is defined as a situation where suspicion arises because of the behaviour of a civilian plane, which could indicate it might be used as a weapon in a terrorist attack.

One can never exclude the possibility of such a threat, or as Schóber et. Al. (2012: 95) put it when discussing QRA and renegades: "(...) terrorism is considered to be the most serious threat to air transport. Many agree that this threat is real, persistent, evolving, sophisticated and hardly predictable. Terrorists use asymmetric methods which are difficult to reveal and defend against them".

Whereas QRA is strongly embedded in NATO, renegades are a purely national matter, decided by the 'National Governmental Authority' (NGA). The same fighter jets are used, but NATO has no say about renegades. An important reason is the ethical aspect inherent in the threat of a renegade: terrorists have hijacked a civilian plane and want to use it to cause massive damage on the ground. If a government wants to eliminate this threat, it might have to shoot down the plane and kill scores of innocent civilians. Consequently, the matter becomes a question of numbers: is a government willing to kill a certain number of civilians in order to save others (probably more) on the ground?

This is a question that each national government has to answer for itself, but it is important that there is an answer before the situation ever takes place. Because, as Edwards (2007: 135-136) remarks: "There is a huge challenge involved in correctly identifying a renegade aircraft. Intentions of the pilots are almost always ambiguous, and combined with the speed of the aircraft make positive determination of a threat and the opportunity to respond nearly impossible. [...] ROE must clearly state who has the authority who has the authority to order the shoot down of a civil aircraft, and under what circumstances".

Belgium and the Netherlands allow for the possibility of lethal violence. They have trained pilots for this scenario, because the pilot cannot hesitate if he is ordered to shoot (by the Dutch or Belgian government) (Lijnen, 2014). In Belgium, the Minister of Defence gives the final order, but he must consult with the

Prime Minister and the Minister of the Interior[25]. In the Netherlands, the minister of Justice makes this decision. Other countries have explicitly chosen to exclude lethal violence; Germany for example adopted a law in 2005 that would allow for the possibility of shooting down a renegade, but the Constitutional Court later deemed this measure unconstitutional, since the Constitution forbids the German state to kill any civilian (Edwards, 2007: 135)[26].

Luxemburg has also forbidden lethal violence. Given that Luxemburg is a signatory to the Benelux Air Defence Pact, this means that Belgian or Dutch pilots will intercept suspicious airplanes under QRA and renegade procedures, but they cannot shoot down a renegade as long as it flies over Luxemburg (or hypothetically, when the renegade dives towards the ground).

Conclusion

The Benelux countries have historically been driving forces towards stronger European cooperation and

---

[25] Swift communication is essential in this scenario. A conference call will be made between the Belgian ministers, which has already been exercised twice according to a government official (Belgische Kamer van Volksvertegenwoordigers, 2016b: 6).

[26] The German Federal Court reportedly wants to reintroduce the possibility of lethal violence (World Bulletin, 2014).

integration. The Benelux Air Defence Pact is the first of its kind. It is unseen that for example a Dutch minister instructs a Belgian pilot to use lethal violence, let alone against a target which contains civilians. This cooperation allows for coordination, information exchange and further mutual trust building. It should drive operational costs down for all parties involved, since they can share the fighter jets that are needed to guard the collective airspace.

A renegade can never be deemed impossible, which forces national governments to decide beforehand if lethal violence could be used. This decision and the operational procedures remain a national, sovereign matter, yet its final execution can be performed by either Dutch or Belgian pilots, whichever happens to be on duty.

All countries involved seem to have realised that they are not giving up their national sovereignty. In fact, their sovereignty is strengthened, even if their national autonomy is somewhat weakened, because this cooperation allows for enhanced operational abilities. The political process that preceded this Pact, which began in 2004, shows how long the formation of such structures can take. This should not leave us in desolation, but rather with the realisation that projects for more European Defence cooperation should be set in motion today, rather than tomorrow.

References:

Belgische Kamer van Volksvertegenwoordigers (2015a) 'Wetsontwerp houdende instemming met het Akkoord tussen de Regering van het Koninkrijk België en de Regering van de Franse Republiek betreffende de samenwerking inzake luchtverdediging tegen niet-militaire luchtdreigingen, gesloten te Tours op 6 juli 2005'. Accessed on February 13, 2016, http://www.dekamer.be/FLWB/PDF/54/1145/54K1 145001.pdf.

Belgische Kamer van Volksvertegenwoordigers (2015b) 'Wetsontwerp houdende instemming met het Akkoord tussen de Regering van het Koninkrijk België en de Regering van de Franse Republiek betreffende de samenwerking inzake luchtverdediging tegen niet-militaire luchtdreigingen, gesloten te Tours op 6 juli 2005. Verslag namens de Commissie voor de Buitenlandse Betrekkingen'. Accessed on February 13, 2016, http://www.dekamer.be/FLWB/PDF/54/1145/54K1 145002.pdf.

Belgische Kamer van Volksvertegenwoordigers (2016a) 'Wetsontwerp houdende instemming met het Akkoord tussen het Koninkrijk België, het Koninkrijk der Nederlanden en het Groothertogdom Luxemburg inzake de integratie van de beveiliging van het luchtruim tegen dreigingen die uitgaan van niet-militaire luchtvaartuigen (renegades), gedaan te 's Gravenhage op 4 maart 2015'. Accessed on February 12, 2016, http://www.dekamer.be/FLWB/PDF/54/1575/54K1575001.pdf.

Belgische Kamer van Volksvertegenwoordigers (2016b) 'Wetsontwerp houdende instemming met het Akkoord tussen het Koninkrijk België, het Koninkrijk der Nederlanden en het Groothertogdom Luxemburg inzake de integratie van de beveiliging van het luchtruim tegen dreigingen die uitgaan van niet-militaire luchtvaartuigen (renegades), gedaan te 's-Gravenhage op 4 maart 2015. Verslag namens de Commissie voor de Buitenlandse Betrekkingen'. Accessed on February 13, 2016 http://www.dekamer.be/FLWB/PDF/54/1575/54K1575002.pdf.

Defensie.nl 'Vliegtuigen onderscheppen'. Accessed on February 13, 2016, https://www.defensie.nl/onderwerpen/verdediging-nederlands-luchtruim/inhoud/vliegtuigen-onderscheppen.

Edwards, Jonathan P. (2007) 'The Law and Rules of Engagement Against Suicide Attacks'. In: *Suicide as a Weapon*. Nato Science for Peace and Security Studies, Vol. 30. Amsterdam, IOS Press.

Lijnen, Nele (2014) 'Schriftelijke vraag nr. 5-11131 van Nele Lijnen (Open Vld) d.d. 14 februari 2014 aan de vice-eersteminister en minister van Landsverdediging'. Accessed on February 13, 2016, http://www.senate.be/www/?MIval=/Vragen/Schrift elijkeVraag&LEG=5&NR=11131&LANG=nl.

Schóber et. Al. (2012) 'Possibilities of countering the air threat and prevention against it'. *Management and Socio-Humanities.*

World Bulletin (2014) 'German court to permiss shooting down of hijacked planes '. Accessed on February 13, 2016, http://www.worldbulletin.net/terrorism/133197/ge rman-court-to-permiss-shooting-down-of-hijacked-planes.

KATALIN CSEH
NATO's Strategic Perspective: Rising Challenges in the East

The focus of this essay is on NATO's strategic perspective regarding rising challenges on its eastern flank. The strategic context in which NATO operates, the political and military implications for the Alliance, and its broader strategic concept and political guidance needs to be considered. Discussion centres largely on Ukraine and Russia and focuses simultaneously on ensuring NATO's collective security, defending the values of NATO countries, and attempting to avoid military escalation. Significant debate centres on NATO's inherent mission and how its response to the Ukraine crisis should depend on whether NATO is a values-based organisation or merely a collective security alliance.

Strategic priorities/objectives: "how might we..."

• Pose a greater viable conventional military deterrent?

• Forge a consensus among NATO members of NATO threats?

• Address nonconventional threats in the east?

- More effectively coordinate with other organisations?

The responses are to increase and adjust NATO policy and interoperability to further cooperation, focus on areas of common interest with Russia, and increase NATO's military readiness and military cooperation.

Recommended Actions:

Increase and adjust NATO policy and interoperability to further cooperation.

Focus on spending NATO's money more effectively. A financial-cooperation escalation is necessary over approximately 20 years, with joint research and development (R&D) and technology funding in five years, target spending areas for members in fifteen years, and joint procurement in twenty years. Some major challenges would be sovereignty concerns, protests from military production firms, and the varying desires and requirements of specific militaries.

However, there are also myriad benefits to this strategy, including saving resources over the long run, avoiding duplication, deployment of the best technologies, efficient resource use, interoperability, and mission-focused investment. I can be concluded that, while profits would remain the main driver of the military-industrial complex, the creation of transatlantic military-industrial champions — "super-contractors," or transatlantic contractor associations with enforced common standards— would account for the scope and commonality needed for economies of scale. This would lead to a decrease in the number of platforms, and reduce duplication of efforts and materials. The reduction in platforms would make logistics easier, as fewer types of parts would require distribution. Moreover, this reduction in platforms would automatically ensure interoperability between hardware.

The transatlantic military-industrial champions would then have the capacity to channel multiple states' R&D spending into the priorities of their clients, while serving the interests of NATO. A final, serious issue that NATO must face is parochialism, which remains a major concern in defence contracting. In order for these reforms to succeed, there needs to be a commitment to open bidding across the Alliance by defence contractors for all NATO contracts.

This may help to avoid protests from the military-industrial complex and assuage fears that large American and British defence contractors could dominate the process. In addition, some form of commitment that no single company can hold more than a certain proportion of contracts (e.g., 20-25 percent) would stop the process from being dominated by one or two of the largest companies.

Focus on areas of common interest with Russia

The importance of adhering to NATO's original mission of collective security for its members is paramount. Russia's actions in Ukraine cannot be automatically assumed to predict any future actions it might take with an actual NATO ally; thus, NATO should avoid intervening in the Ukraine crisis militarily. When assessing the situation in Ukraine and wider relations with Russia, it is important to step back and consider the security situation more broadly. NATO has interests in areas where Russia can play a role, such as Iran, North Korea and now forcefully in Syria.

While peace in Europe is paramount, NATO must balance its desire to roll back the Russian position in Ukraine with its desire to prevent further escalation in Europe. A direct conflict between NATO and Russia would lead to greater insecurity in Europe in the near future. Here, it is important to point out, that, collective security only applies to NATO members.

This strategy would allow for much greater cooperation opportunities between NATO and Russia, NATO and the European Union (EU), and the EU and Russia. The points of cooperation might include: violent extremism, Iran, Afghanistan, proliferation of WMDs, trade, and energy policy. A pull-out of Ukraine could be accomplished if NATO takes actions that are reassuring to the existing members of NATO, particularly with regard to military readiness and cooperation. The key would be to maintain robust communication within NATO and to maintain, and in certain cases amplify, its deterrent capacity for current members.

Additionally, all efforts would be made to avoid public relations debacles. A pull-out of Ukraine, without a robust deterrence policy for existing members, would certainly lead to a "loss of face." However, the key is to leave no ambiguity for Russia. If NATO does not expand east, Russia must not move to destabilize present NATO members. A robust expansion of deterrent capacities to reinforce that deal should avoid losing face, at least as it pertains specifically to NATO.

Increase NATO's military readiness and military cooperation

The focus is on deterrence and reassurance, and a permanent rotation of military troops. This policy would solve the problem of western NATO members preferring a rotational presence in Eastern Europe, whilst eastern members want permanent deployments. It would achieve the permanent buy-in of western allies, along with the provision of continued reassurance to NATO's eastern allies. To accomplish this, there must be an easing of restrictions on the transportation of NATO troops and equipment, and exploring of multinational funding.

During this permanent rotation, national troops would operate under the NATO command structure, thereby increasing deterrence and interoperability benefits, and, most importantly, improving battle readiness. In addition, the Alliance should reconsider the deployment of a ballistic-missile-defence system in Poland and the Czech Republic, as originally envisioned. This would bring a degree of greater comfort, particularly to Poland, that the Alliance will remain committed to the defence of Eastern European members. Further, NATO should clarify that it will not only maintain its current tactical nuclear doctrine, but it will also upgrade those capacities to assure their deterrent value.

This upgrade should be clearly articulated as a response to any aggression toward existing NATO members. Transportation by air seems to be the method that would face the lowest hurdles for the rotation. Therefore, the aim would be to transport as much equipment and as many troops as possible by air. If a participating country does not have the necessary airlifting capabilities, then these should be provided by NATO for this task.

Of course, some equipment— such as explosives, heavy armoured units, and artillery—might be difficult to transport by air, so the restrictions for transportation on the ground would also need to be loosened for this particular NATO permanent rotation. It can be concluded that a legislative solution might also be possible. Pressure could be put on national governments to pass legislation that permits freer movement of NATO-assigned troops through Europe.

Given the current threat climate, such legislation might be quite easy to pass. It would also provide a strengthening function for the Alliance, implying that member states trust each other to transport troops across member state borders.

BENJAMIN FIEVET
Europe needs to step up in response to Russia

After the collapse of the Soviet Union and the fall of communism, it seemed that liberalism had prevailed. Western states adapted to the new situation by consolidating the liberal world order and gradually extending membership in its institution (the EU and NATO) to the east.

However, Russia never really integrated in this liberal world and under Vladimir Putin aspires to reclaim its former place on the world stage by practicing realpolitik. Something Europeans have failed to understand with worrisome consequences for their defence apparatus.

Naturally, Putin's has been exploiting this incomprehension and the weaknesses that ensued. Europe now needs to start playing the same game as its adversary and send a clear signal that it is united as well as willing and able to defend its interests by itself.

Putin's realism

If Putin's Russia, as recount Dmitri Trenin, initially tried, in the early 2000's, to integrate itself in the Western world, it didn't last. By 2008, Putin had become frustrated by what he perceived as the West's "scant respect for [Russia's] interests or views".[27] When Putin became President again after Medvedev's term, in 2012, its foreign policy goal became "full sovereignty". As Trenin puts it:

This sovereignty bid, in practical terms, represents Moscow's clear breakout from the international system as it has been widely, if informally, understood since the end of the Cold War. It challenges the unipolar world order both by erecting barriers to U.S. democracy promotion and by refusing to submit to the norms and practices laid down, policed, and arbitrated by the West.[28]

Some argue that Putin's foreign policy is only the consequence of its interior political needs. But Putin, a former KGB officer, has always been nostalgic of the USSR former might and "full of bitterness at how *"the Soviet Union had lost its position in Europe""*.[29] In an

---

[27] Dmitri Trenin, "Russia's Breakout From the Post–Cold War System: The Drivers of Putin's Course", Carnegie Moscow Center, December 22, 2014 http://carnegie.ru/2014/12/22/russia-s-breakout-from-post-cold-war-system-drivers-of-putin-s-course/

[28] Ibid.

[29] Mary Elise Sarotte, 2014 "A Broken Promise?", *Foreign Affairs*, 93(5)

article in Foreign affairs in 2014, John J. Mearsheimer identified what Putin really is: a realist.[30]

Consequently, Putins's disregard for international law –that he sees as the rules imposed by the Western World– and his exploitation of the West weaknesses should come as no surprise.

Russia's resurgence

Since 2014 and the onset of the events in Ukraine, a resurgent Russia has been playing a provocation game. In Ukraine, of course, when it intervened in the affairs of a sovereign state but also with incursions in sovereign waters and airspaces of EU and NATO members. And now in Syria which has turned in a proxy war.

For Gregory Feifer, Russia has been "testing NATO's commitment to collective security".[31] A sentiment echoed by Jeffrey Stacey who says Russia has been "poking and prodding" the West and that the absence

---

[30] John J. Mearsheimer, 2014 "Why the Ukraine Crisis Is the West's Fault", *Foreign Affairs,* 93(5)

[31] Foreign Affairs Unedited, "The Russian Intervention: Putin, NATO, and the Western Response", October 19, 2015, https://www.foreignaffairs.com/audios/2015-10-18/russian-intervention-syria [podcast]

of a forceful reaction is interpreted by Putin as weakness.[32]

Stacey adds that "Western deterrence of Russian projection and use of force has now deteriorated so badly that [he is] concerned that Russia may yet attempt Baltic incursions."[33]

Europe's weakness

Since the end of the cold war, the soviet threat having disappeared, NATO's main mission of collective defence had been relegated behind new roles of crisis management operations and the creation of a network of partners around the globe.[34]

Meanwhile, under a relative sense of security and pushed by financial constraints, European countries have cut their defence budgets and most are now well under the 2% of GDP target of NATO. A level of spending that does not allow them the capability to sustain military operations on their own and put at risk their security. Although Obama[35] and NATO's Jens

---

[32] Ibid.

[33] Ibid.

[34] Ibid.

[35] White House, "Remarks by President Obama at 25th Anniversary of Freedom Day—Warsaw, Poland," June 4, 2014,

Stoltenberg[36] have repeatedly assured that NATO would protect its members, there is cause for concern. A Pew Research Center's survey found that –with the exception of the US and Canada– a minority of people in every other NATO member state would support a military intervention to defend a NATO ally in a conflict with Russia.[37] This raises questions about the political will of European countries to act in the case of such an event.

Even as the United States have operated an Asia pivot and indicated several times to European countries that they should become security producers and not just security consumers, Europeans NATO members seem to rely solely on the United States to ensure their security under Article 5 of the Treaty. Something confirmed, recently, at the Munich Security Conference during which "the call for greater American leadership

www.whitehouse.gov/the-press-office/2014/06/04/remarks-president-obama-25th-anniversary-freedom-day-warsaw-poland

[36] "Session at the Brussels Forum with participation of NATO Secretary General Jens Stoltenberg" March 20, 2015 http://www.nato.int/cps/en/natohq/opinions_118347.htm

[37] Pew Research Center, "NATO Public Opinion: Wary of Russia, Leery of Action on Ukraine", June 10, 2015, http://www.pewglobal.org/2015/06/10/1-nato-public-opinion-wary-of-russia-leary-of-action-on-ukraine/

was a constant" according to Richard Fontaine.[38] Another way to say it would be that Europeans, as a whole, are not taking their security seriously enough since they refuse to take charge of it.

If, in reaction to the recent events, the United States have announced –the same day as the publication of a report stating that Russia could conquer Estonia and Latvia in three days–[39] that they would quadruple their military spending in Europe,[40] it is not enough and should not give Europe a reason to postpone what is necessary: a European Defence Union.

The European Union needs to step up its game

If Europe is to stay true to its liberal values, it can't let Putin's Russia impose its will on other countries by force. But to respond adequately, it needs to recognize

---

[38] Richard Fontaine, "Doom and Gloom: Five Key Takeaways from the Munich Security Conference", *War on the Rocks*, February 16, 2016, http://warontherocks.com/2016/02/doom-and-gloom-five-key-takeaways-from-the-munich-security-conference/

[39] Robert Beckhusen, "Russia Needs Three Days to Conquer Estonia and Latvia" *War Is Boring*, February 5, 2016, http://warisboring.com/articles/russia-needs-three-days-to-conquer-estonia-and-latvia/

[40] Andrew Rettman, "US to quadruple military spending in Europe", *EU Observer*, February 2, 2016, https://euobserver.com/foreign/132101

that Putin is not a liberal and will not accept the rules of liberalism. He is thinking in terms of hard power and Europe needs to respond the same way if it wants its message to be received. Europe's responses to Russia's actions must become more vigorous and not shy away from the use of force if necessary.

Even though NATO is traditionally tasked with the collective defence of Europe, not all EU members are NATO members. A fully integrated European Army not being immediately possible, European units, originally tasked with territorial defence of the EU –other tasks could be added–, should be created with troops directly under EU control. This would require the creation of a permanent Operational Headquarter as well as a European defence budget.

Additionally, member States need to reinforce cooperation at the operational and industrial level and a common strategy needs to be set for the EU. Such measures, far from competing with NATO, would show the United States that Europe is interested in its own defence and can become a security provider and a real partner.

MAXIMILIAN HEILMANN
A European strategy to tackle new methods of war.
The European Single Army

At times after the cold war is the European Union tackled by new challenges. Especially after the intervention in the Ukraine and the annexation of the Krim by Russia, the times have changed. Both sides, the NATO states and Russia, are performing a deliberate provocation on the borders of the European Union.

"[If we are having a closer look to the enlargement of the NATO states we see that] Bulgaria, Estonia, Latvia, Lithuania, Romania, Slovakia, and Slovenia joined [in 2004], followed in 2009 by Albania and Croatia. Those enlargements upset Russia." (Dempsey, 2014)

On the other hand, are the military interventions in Ukraine and the entering NATO Airspace with military airplanes by the Russians a significant sign for a showdown between Russia and the western society.

"A United States military spokesman, Col. Steven Warren, confirmed [...] that Turkish pilots had warned the Russian pilot 10 times, but that the Russian jet ignored the warnings." (MacFarquhar & Erlanger, 2015)

Therefore, we can assume that the Russian Jet entered the NATO Airspace by purpose, what makes the situation even more complicated. This specific example shows us, that we have entered into a decade of provocation between Russia and the NATO States. The European Union and the NATO states have to take into account, that we should interact with one voice, not only on the diplomatic level. Therefore, we have to call for a deeper cooperation between member states and the national armed forces in the short them and move over to a united Army in the long term.

Beside the crisis with Russia are much more reasons who are calling for deeper cooperation. The refugee crisis and the pirates over takings showed us that our Military has to work more together. Each strength of each national Army should be used in the best order. But if we look to the future, a Single European Force would be a suitable solution. Especially for the long-term, we as the European Union has to extend strengths and minimize weaknesses within our Army Forces.

The Single European Army a sign for an Integration

Every national army force is specialised on different fields of interaction. Especially while the northern European Counties are focused on maritime interaction got other states more active in the air force.

Or also smaller states like Estonia, focused on different fields like cyber-war.

"Juncker [...] said, getting member states to combine militarily would make spending more efficient and would encourage further European integration." (Sparrow, 2015)

Moreover, a single European Army would get the second largest Army field in the whole world. This means that the European Union no longer has the need to rely on the support of the US-Army. This gives European Countries more independence regarding interactions in global missions.

Multinational conflicts have to be handled by multinational Army

Another important point is that, very small army forces like those who exists in the Baltics or other small eastern European countries are not able to interact suitable to the menaces of the current global position.

"The past proved that missions like the ones in Kosovo and Afghanistan are possible when a crisis becomes urgent, even if there are various national reservations and strategic disagreements. This is why the German federal government supports the model of pooling and sharing. This type of cooperation also comes as an aftermath of the financial crisis: in recent years, defence budgets declined all across Europe. So in 2010 the

member states decided to pool and share, aiming to save money as well as be more efficient." (Jung, 2014)

The member states should work in the long-term perspective, regarding the sharing and caring principle. With such a strategy, we are getting more efficient and improve the effectiveness of interactions. Current political problems like in the Ukraine or in the middle east cannot be solved by small national army forces. These conflicts lead us to new dimensions of intervention measurements, which are calling for more cooperation and collaboration within the European forces.

European national forces are no longer up to date with their technical equipment. Planes from the Air Force of Eastern European countries are sometimes older than 25 Years and are relics of the USSR. With a European Army the EU would not only be able to centralize the commanders to Brussels, we would be able to centralize the coordination of replacements of old equipment by new once as well.

Cost benefits of a new common Army structure

Crew training could be centralized and also save money for every member state. Moreover, the coordination of interactions could be much easier, because instructions can be delivered to the forces directly by the European headquarter. It would be not necessary that ongoing procedures get ratified by each national army. Such a headquarter has to be created internationally and should represent the values of the European member states. Another important point is the reduction of the total spending by deeper cooperation.

"For the development of future military capabilities could be embraced. Such a concept computes savings and costs from EU cooperation into procurement decisions and thus fosters further EU-wide collaboration and efficiency." (Rogers & Gilli, 2013)

Until now, as Figure 1 shows, every member state has a different amount of spending in army forces. Minimization of the costs and a maximizing of the effectiveness would lead us towards a strong and highly developed modern army. The statistics show us the expenses for the military in NATO states.

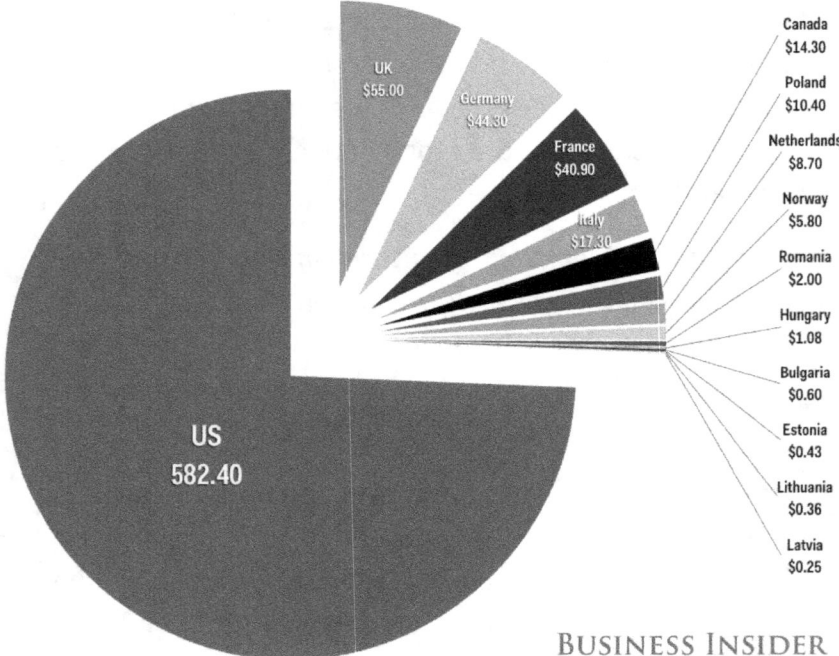

NATO members' military expenditure in billions of US dollars, 2014

UK
$55.00

Germany
$44.30

France
$40.90

Italy
$17.30

US
582.40

Canada
$14.30

Poland
$10.40

Netherlands
$8.70

Norway
$5.80

Romania
$2.00

Hungary
$1.08

Bulgaria
$0.60

Estonia
$0.43

Lithuania
$0.36

Latvia
$0.25

BUSINESS INSIDER

(Business Insider, 2015)

What we can see is that the USA is with a spending of 582,4 billion of US-Dollars the leader within the NATO states, regarding the total spending. But regarding the deep cooperation's could the European States with a total spending of 187,12 work in a more efficient way than other armed forces.

Conclusion

To create United European forces would be a long-term process, which will start in the first step with a deeper cooperation between the as long national forces. In the long-term it is important to get over to European Force, which will coordinate by the European Union. We have to reduce bureaucratic obstacles. Those regulations are preventing deeper cooperation and impede the first steps for an Army of the European Union, which would be more modern and cost-efficient than the current national once.

References:

Dempsey, J. (2014, June 24). Why Defence Matters: A New Narrative for NATO. Retrieved from Carnegie Europe:
http://carnegieeurope.eu/publications/?fa=55979#

Jung, F. (2014, April 14). Dual force. Retrieved from TheEuropean.eu: http://en.theeuropean.eu/franz-josef-jung--3/8280-european-army-a-vision-for-the-future

MacFarquhar, N., & Erlanger, S. (2015, November 24). NATO-Russia Tensions Rise After Turkey Downs Jet. Retrieved from The New York Times:
http://www.nytimes.com/2015/11/25/world/europe/turkey-syria-russia-military-plane.html?_r=0

Rogers, J., & Gilli, A. (2013, May). Enabling the furture: European military capabilities 2013-2025: challenges and avenues. Retrieved from Issue: http://www.iss.europa.eu/uploads/media/Report_16 .pdf

Sparrow, A. (2015, March 8). Jean-Claude Juncker calls for EU army. Retrieved from TheGuardian: http://www.theguardian.com/world/2015/mar/08/j ean-claude-juncker-calls-for-eu-army-european-commission-miltary

Pictures:

Business Insider (2015 February 26). This is how much NATO member states spend on their military. Retrieved from UK Business Insider: http://uk.businessinsider.com/how-much-every-nato-member-spends-on-military-in-2014-2015-2

EMMA JANSON
The Need for European Military Cooperation

A hundred years ago the First World War had broken out, after the first shot was fired in Europe. Young men sacrificed their lives on the battlefields and the war ended with a death toll higher, much thanks to new technology, than ever recorded before. The League of Nations was formed and we said the world should cooperate and make sure this never happened again. We all know the history following this.

A Second World War, with even greater technological advancements and even greater death tolls came. And following it came a prolonged Cold war, a war in technological advancements that never really broke out to a third warm world war because nobody believed we would survive the new weapons where they all to be used. After years of competition, due to political and economic reasons, the Cold war ended when one of the sides collapsed.

Since the end of the Cold war we have seen smaller wars, in Europe and outside of it, horrific wars but never really threatening to evolve in to major world wars. The west has sometimes sent enforcements or even been initiating the wars but the thought of another war on a western country's soil seems unthinkable.

The belief of end of history was formed. After the Cold war ended more and more countries signed up to the liberal and democratic ideas of the west and we wanted to believe that one day the world would be made up solely of democracies and the peaceful world we all long for would soon arrive.

Whilst we now see that the end of history is far away, the western countries still handle their militaries as if this was not the case. It is like the fact that no two democracies have never gone in to war with each other has not just lead to the idea that it is impossible for a democracy to ever attack another in the future, it also seems to have shaped the idea that a democracy can never be attacked.

Unfortunately, we have seen lately that this might not be the case. It has been over a decade since the US was shocked by its first major terrorist attack in New York. Is has been no more than a couple of months since Europe and Paris was shocked by its latest terrorist attack. The military is back on the streets in Europe and the idea of the untouchable democracies is starting to crumble.

If there is a new great war coming in the future the first shot might not be fired in Europe this time, given the great job the European Union has done in shaping mutual trust and solidarity between the European nations, but that doesn't mean Europe will remain unaffected.

We hear talk about a shift towards a multi-polar world order, but this seems to be only viewed through economic and political analysis, less often do we hear about a shift of military might. If we look too military spending it might be true that the US is spending 570$bn and the European countries are spending about 260$bn Turkey 16$bn, this whilst Russia is spending 53$bn, China 190$bn, India 50$bn Saudi Arabia 46$bn and Japan 49$bn[1].

This does not look too dim, but it is also in relation to the fact that all the western countries are decreasing their spending whilst other are increasing[2]. Also, spending does not necessarily reflect the efficiency of the military. If we look to the European nations and the US, Europe is spending 45% of the US budget whilst we are only 10-15% as efficient[3].

European nations are not terrible at spending on their militaries, even if NATO is somewhat upset by the fact that few countries today are living up to their 2% of GDP commitment. But much of our spending is focused on keeping old equipment alive rather than investing in new. We have seen a lot of examples of this. If we look to Germany who has one of the major armies in

Europe only 24 out of 56 trooper planes works, 16 of 83 helicopters are in fighting condition, when they sent patriot missiles to Turkey for their defence against Syria only half of the stock was functioning.

This is not unique to Germany, on the other side of the Atlantic the average age of the American warplanes is now 42 years and their stock has halved since the end of the Cold war. When NATO went in to Libya in 2011 they were short in correctly trained personnel and short in equipment, only after a few weeks the European countries had to turn to the US for new artilleries.

There is a hollowing out of the western armies where they look strong on paper but where large parts are not in fighting condition and where there is a lack of military personnel training[4]. This can only be solved by every country taking a through look at how their military budget is being spent and by trying to make this spending more efficient.

There is a hollowing out of the military equipment in the western countries, but this does not explain why the US is so much more efficient than the European countries. One major explanation is the fact that the US is one country with one army while Europe is many countries and every country has their own army. It is more difficult to coordinate when different troops have different heads of states that gives them different criteria's to work by; it is also more difficult to coordinate troops who does not speak the same language or have the same cultural backgrounds.

One other major explanation is that since the Cold war ended we also lost the common enemy. When the Soviet collapsed, we lost part of the initiative for cooperation. The threat was no longer immediate and the NATO member started to loosen up and move funding from the military to other aspects of the national needs.

Today we see new threats, but depending on geographical location countries tends to focus on different threats. Whilst the Balkan and Eastern European countries are growing weary of a more aggressive Russia, countries in the south of Europe such as Spain and Italy are more worried about the Middle Eastern conflicts. Many of the European countries are still keeping their military spending below the NATO 2%. This is partly because they rely on the US for salvation come conflict, though this is not certain given the many hotspots the US is now keeping an eye on in the global arena of conflicts. Partly because they do no longer rely on their European neighbours to lend helping hands when they do not share the same threat. Military cooperation between the western countries is taking a turn for the worse, turning in to an opt-in alliance rather than a sound alliance based on genuine solidarity[5]. This must change, the European countries are closer than ever thanks to the great work of the European Union and it must be a given that we will help our friends if they are in need. All members of NATO must be able to rely on the article 5. All members of the EU must be able to rely on the Solidarity clause. In a world of unrest, it is extremely important to be willing to stand up for and defend our common values, both in words and in action.

We have seen that the western world is not immune to attacks. The liberal, democratic Europe is not immune to harm. It is about time the European nations start to take their military cooperation seriously again. Be it via NATO or via EU. We need solidarity and we need the ability to defend our values and our valuable democracies. More dedication, cooperation and solidarity are greatly needed. Europe is always stronger united.

References:

1.http://www.businessinsider.com/the-largest-defence-budgets-in-the-world-2015-10?IR=T

2.http://www.economist.com/news/economic-and-financial-indicators/21643167-global-defence-spending

3.file:///Users/Emma/Downloads/ALDE%20Roadm ap%20-%20EU%20INTEGRATED%20MILITARY%20FORCES %20-%20Defence-Paper-EN-FR.pdf

4.http://www.bbc.co.uk/programmes/b05qgd0n

5.http://carnegieeurope.eu/publications/?fa=55979#

JORGE DE JESUS
European Defence and Security: North Africa and the Sahel

The Paris attacks of the 13th November 2015, which were a tragedy not only for the people of France but for whole of the European Union, illustrated the grave problems that currently exist in the sphere of defence and security within the EU. Our immediate neighbourhood is drowning under the weight of terrorism and oppression, our external borders and the individual security forces of each member state are unable to protect our homeland, and our citizens fall victim to this chaos both at home and abroad.

While the EU remains focused on ISIS, the war in Syria and Iraq and resulting refugee crisis, its strategy towards North Africa and the Sahel has reflected a grave desynchronization of threat perception between the member states, and a lack of willingness to act in a meaningful manner.

This strategy, or lack thereof, has perpetuated an environment fertile for terrorism and criminal activity which poses a grave threat to the Union and its interests. Only by synchronizing threat perceptions and by unifying the defence and security apparatus of the EU's member states can we pacify and stabilize the region and ensure the defence of European citizens.

North Africa and the Sahel is a region fraught with socio-economic problems and weak political governance. This situation has transformed the region into a breeding ground for trafficking, Islamic terrorism and illegal migration, all which have been exacerbated by the fall of the Ghaddafi regime in Libya in 2011 (Korteweg 2014: 252-53).

The threat to Europe's defence and security is two-fold: firstly, illegal migration across the Central Mediterranean Route from Libya into Italy has placed a great burden not only on Italy, but on the entire Union, and has led to a tremendous loss of life. In 2014-15, a total of 324,706 immigrants made their way into the EU through this route (FRONTEX 2016). The flow of refugees from this area predates the boom experienced in the summer of 2015 from the Middle East, and its continuation reflects a clear failure of European policy in dealing with the problem.

Secondly, the region is fertile ground for Islamic terrorism, which has not only shown very little signs of abating, but it has also systematically targeted European citizens and interests in the region. One of biggest perpetrators is Al-Qaeda in the Islamic Maghreb (AQIM), which has been responsible for a variety attacks such as the 2015 hotel attack in

Bamako, Mali, as well as this year's attacks in Ouagadougou, Burkina Faso (both done in collaboration with Al-Mourabitoun, an AQIM splinter group). Both attacks left scores of Europeans, among others, dead. AQIM is also notable for its recent involvement in the Northern Mali uprising, which it used to further consolidate its position (National Counterterrorism Centre 2016). The Al-Mourabitoun, for its part, was responsible for the In Amenas hostage crisis in Algeria in 2013, which resulted in over 60 deaths, 37 of which were civilians.

The threat of terrorist attacks against European targets is exacerbated by the growing fragmentation and decentralization of terrorist activity, a reality which has allowed the Islamic State to extend its activities into North Africa and the Sahel. ISIS claimed responsibility for the Bardo National Museum Attack in Tunis, 2015, which led to the deaths of a total of 21 people, 18 of which were tourists, among them European citizens (El-Ghobashy and Addala 2015).

Further attacks claimed by ISIS in the region include the mass shooting in Sousse, Tunisia in 2015, resulting in the deaths of 37 Europeans (Addala and El-Ghobashy 2015). The Islamic State has also been allowed to establish a presence in Libya, from which they could feasibly also carry out attacks on European soil.

Concerted European action aimed at tackling the threats that originate in North Africa and the Sahel has been far from satisfactory. The pivot from regionalism to bilateralism in EU-North Africa relations, as exemplified by the creation of the Union for the Mediterranean in 2008, and the depoliticization of issues such as human rights, represents a setback to any development previously made by the 1995 Euro-Mediterranean Partnership (Bicchi 2011). EU missions in the area include the EU Training Mission-Mali, launched in 2013 upon the request of Mali, as well as two CSDP missions: EUCAP Sahel Niger (2012 – present) and EUCAP Sahel Mali (2015 – present) (European Council 2015).

While the true effectiveness of these missions can only be properly determined in years to come, we can say they have so far not done enough to actively counter the threat of Islamic terrorism. In Libya, the EU Border Assistance Mission has all but failed (EEAS 2015), and the political process to form a unity government has taken so long that ISIS has acquired a strong foothold in the country.

As a result, the defence of Europe and its citizens has been left in the hands of individual countries, both EU member states and those in the region. France is the only EU member state who seems to realise the importance of maintaining stability in the Maghreb and the Sahel. It was France who first intervened in Mali in 2012 to prevent the northern rebellion from turning the country into a terrorist hotspot, and it is France who maintains a force of over 3,000 soldiers on the ground in the Sahel as part of Operation Barkhane (Ministère de la Défence 2016).

While France must be commended on its efforts in the region, and while it is clear that France's connection with the region makes the country particularly suitable for the task, it is clear that uncoordinated strategies followed by individual EU member states will always fall short of being able to fully defend European citizens and stamp out terrorism: they were not enough to prevent the attack on Paris, Mali and Burkina Faso, and will remain unable to prevent future attacks unless there is a change in strategy.

In light of the dire threat to European security and interests originating in North Africa and the Sahel, what can the Union do to defend its citizens and pacify the region? The solution to this crucial defence and security problem requires, at first instance, a two-fold approach that deals with, primarily, the issue of diverging threat perceptions, and secondly with the lack of EU hard power.

The divergence of threat perceptions among the different member states of the EU is one of the main obstacles to the development of a coherent EU security and defence policy (Dempsey 2014). So long as different member states continue to priorities different issues, the ability of the EU as a whole to defend its own territory will remain inadequate. The chaos in North Africa and the Sahel is one of the greatest threats to the security of the Union and its citizens.

The existence of ungoverned spaces, coupled with the growing decentralization of terrorism and lack of comprehensive and concerted European action in the area, could mean that the region would remain a terrorist hotspot long after ISIS has been defeated in the Middle East. It is thus of paramount importance that the EU as a whole realise that the North Africa-Sahel region is not of secondary importance to the war on terror, but rather a central theatre that deserves as much attention as the Middle East and Afghanistan, and it must therefore take active steps to put an end to terrorism there.

The EU's strategy in the region should be modelled on the successful comprehensive approach undertaken in the Gulf of Aden. While the EUTM-Mali and the EUCAP mission in Mali and Niger will remain an important part of this approach, it needs to be coupled with European hard power, which represents the second part of our proposed approach. France, for all its effort, cannot be responsible for the defence of the entire continent; it represents an unjust burden on the French society and on its armed forces. EU member states must take active steps to either unite their defence and security apparatus, or pool together resources and troops in a more permanent manner. Many challenges will certainly arise from the creation of such defensive union, challenges which to some may seem insurmountable, and many might object to the mere proposal of such an initiative. However, the situation in the North Africa-Sahel region cannot wait for the European system to come to a conclusion on the matter. Thus, we propose that the first step to acting in the region should be the formation of a coalition of the willing, external to the NATO structure and thus not dependent on US strategic priorities, but rather on European ones.

The creation of a defence union should nonetheless remain a key goal for the EU, and it is undoubtedly the best system through which to act in the North Africa-Sahel region. This hard power would allow the Union to more effectively counter the various threats it faces and to better defend its peoples. The permanent nature of such a force, would ensure that the defence of the Union does not suffer from the issue of free-riding by member states, and it would also not be subject to the whims of transitory governments. In addition, it would also ensure that the EU does not remain dependent on NATO and the paramount role that the USA plays in the defence of the continent. The USA's strategic pivot towards the Asia-Pacific region means the EU must step up its own defence (Dempsey 2014). This is especially important in North Africa and the Sahel.

Overall, the European Union must take advantage of the multiple crises it is currently facing to reform itself in a way that better serves the needs and security of its citizens. This will require a more active approach to North Africa and the Sahel, an area which has become a hotbed for Islamic terrorism and which has resulted in the deaths of scores of Europeans and non-Europeans. It also requires the realization that the Union desperately needs to complement its current approach with a degree of hard power that will allow it to independently counter the multiple threats it faces now and will continue to face in years to come.

References:

Addala and El-Ghobashy 2015. 'Gunman Leaves Dozens Dead at Tunisia Hotel', Wall Street Journal (New York), 27 June 2015

Bicchi, F. 2011. 'The Union for the Mediterranean, or the Changing Context of Euro-Mediterranean Relations', Mediterranean Politics, Vol.16(01), pp.3-19, DOI: 10.1080/13629395.2011.547365

Dempsey, J. 2014. 'Why Defence Matters: A New Narrative for NATO', Carnegie Europe, Available at: http://carnegieeurope.eu/publications/?fa=55979

EEAS 2015. "EU Integrated Border Assistance Mission in Libya (EUBAM Libya)". European Union External Action Service, Common Security and Defence Policy. January 2015. http://eeas.europa.eu/csdp/missions-and-operations/eubam-libya/pdf/factsheet_eubam_libya_en.pdf

El-Ghobashy and Addala, 2015. 'Islamic State Claims Tunis Museum Attack', Wall Street Journal (New York), 20 March 2015

European Council 2015. 'The European Union and the Sahel.' Available at: http://www.consilium.europa.eu/en/workarea/downloadAsset.aspx?id=40802195592

FRONTEX 2016. 'Central Mediterranean Route'. Available at: http://frontex.europa.eu/trends-and-routes/central-mediterranean-route/

Korteweg, R. 2014. 'Treacherous Sands: the EU and terrorism in the broader Sahel'. European Review, Vol.13(2), pp.251-258, DOI 10.1007/s12290-014-0327-1

Ministère de la Défence 2016. 'Opération Barkhane', France. Available at:

http://www.defence.gouv.fr/operations/sahel/dossier-de-presentation-de-l-operation-barkhane/operation-barkhane

National Counterterrorism Centre 2016. 'Al-Qa'ida in the Lands of the Islamic Maghreb (AQIM)'. Available at: http://www.nctc.gov/site/groups/aqim.html

LINA KARKLINA
Europe's Security:
The Role of EU and NATO
Between Europe's East and South

Some describe the current security challenges in Europe as sudden, some claim that the threats we face today were or could have been foreknown and even prevented. Whatever the arguments, no one can deny today the seriousness of the security situation in Europe is or should be dealing with. The threats coming from Russia in Europe's East, the rise of Daesh and the European migrant crisis are the key issues Europe is facing as a continent today. However, it does not necessarily mean that these threats are perceived as equally important in different parts of Europe, namely Europe's East and South, therefore complicating taking actions against them.

European Union's Common Foreign and Security Policy (CFSP) and especially its Common Security and Defence Policy (CSDP) has been widely criticised for its inability to cope with the rising threats and crisis it has caused. As Professor André Gerrits, who specializes in Russian History and Politics at Leiden University said in a conference devoted to EU's CFSP and the current situation in Ukraine, "EU is known to be an economic giant, a political dwarf and a military worm"[41]. He argued that EU has very limited capabilities in foreign policy and even more importantly, divergent interests. This, he claims, is especially evident in EU's relationship with Russia as it is very much influenced by the economic interests of individual member states as well as energy dependency.[42]

The same applies for the EU's response to the current migrant crisis. Juliane Schmidt, Junior Policy from the European Policy Centre (EPC) has looked into this in her policy paper "Seeing the bigger picture: The refugee crisis and the link to CFSP"[43], where she argues that "The EU's current approach in dealing with the refugee crisis is not working" and stresses that "As for the EU's foreign policy response, instead of insisting on fragmented state-level policies, a common approach is required."[44] This is, of course, nothing new and although we have taken steps towards more cooperation and coordination, it is still far from the

---

[41]http://www.atlcom.nl/upload/Report_Meeting_EU_and_Ukraine_1 4-05-2014_def.pdf

[42]http://www.atlcom.nl/upload/Report_Meeting_EU_and_Ukraine_1 4-05-2014_def.pdf

[43] http://www.epc.eu/pub_details.php?cat_id=4&pub_id=6110

[44] http://www.epc.eu/pub_details.php?cat_id=4&pub_id=6110

ideal that we could feel safe in our countries because EU is there to protect us.

That, however, is the main aim of the North Atlantic Treaty Organisation (NATO), or as they put it, "NATO's essential purpose is to safeguard the freedom and security of its members through political and military means."[45] The transatlantic dimension, American leadership and most importantly the principle of collective defence or Article 5 are some of the features than make NATO more trustable in terms of securing the peace in our continent.

With the 27th NATO summit approaching on 8 and 9 July in Warsaw, it is being presumed that the challenges in Europe's East and South will be the priorities of this year's meeting alongside with the necessary reforms in NATO's partnership policy, NATO enlargement to the East and possibly to the North as well as the future of nuclear deterrence. In addition to these challenges, NATO too is struggling with unity and prioritizing. NATO has 28 members at present, from which 22 are European Union member states, therefore focusing on current challenges, the spotlight will be divided between Europe's East and South. In addition to that, unknown are also the prospects for the Transatlantic cooperation and the involvement of

---

[45] http://www.nato.int/nato-welcome/

the United States in the region, taking into account the presidential elections coming up on November 8 this year. The result and its implications for the transatlantic cooperation are very much unclear.

All these issues, together with such aspects as possible EU Brexit, declining defence budgets, unclear Russia's interests in the region and globally, and the politics of individual EU and NATO member states, make the aim of coherent and effective European security and defence policy extremely hard to achieve. Moreover, it is clear that at this point not only the unity of both EU and NATO are at stake, but perhaps even their survival. In this sense the very existence of these organisations should be a priority of its members, therefore significantly influencing their national policies.

This should apply also for the East – South division of security needs in Europe. Russia's military assertiveness and growing security threats in Europe's East have raised significant attention to the region through the military support and reassurance of NATO as well as the diplomatic means and sanctions of EU. Although, one could argue, it is not enough and has not solved the problem, these steps have been important in both reassuring security of, for example, Baltic States. Moreover, European Union has played a significant role in de-escalating the conflict and keeping the door open for negotiations. At the same time, while Europe is focusing on its East, it might rise some concern between southern European countries in regard to their own security priorities in North Africa.

Unlike the pretty straight forward problem in East, the southern block has security problems that are a bit more complex, or harder to define. Migration pressures, instability to the North Africa as well as the rise of extreme groups just over the seas is a crucial yet blurry problem to solve, especially in times of divided focus and security needs in the region. In order to develop a truly coherent and sustainable security strategy of both EU CFSP and NATO, it is important not to ignore or misjudge any of the region's immediate and long-term needs.

Moreover, it is in the interest of both regions and the unity of both organisations to develop a close cooperation and deep understanding between Europe's South and East. It can be developed through an enhanced dialogue between the two regions, perhaps through a separate forum or program, strengthening the military cooperation and assistance through exchanging best practices, cooperating in missions and supporting each other's military capabilities. Finally, NATO and EU should play a significant role in building and supporting this cooperation and understanding by carefully shifting the focus on both regions and working on building as many platforms of cooperation as possible. Indeed, this might be one of the key elements of EU and NATO's attempts to regain its unity and effectiveness.

EDGARS LEJNIEKS
What Are the Main Threats to the European Security?

Since the foundation of the European Economic Community, the region has faced many threats and has dealt with them quite sufficiently. Yet, the international order has changed over time and now we could be facing the most crucial time in the modern history of Europe since the World War 2.

The European Union has expanded significantly and has evolved to a level where member states come from different parts of Europe: West and East with totally different cultural backgrounds and historical paths have to come to logical compromise in the decision-making process that would satisfy all interests.

These clashes of different mentalities, priorities, approaches and interests have put a question mark on the project of European Union. The author of this essay will point out the biggest security threats to Europe and provide some reasoning on why it is important to tackle and handle these issues in order to avoid the collapse of the European Union.

Terrorism

Terrorism obviously goes hand in hand with the refugee crisis. Terrorism is a violence which puts lives at risk; it imposes large costs; it seeks to undermine the openness and tolerance of our societies, and it poses a growing strategic threat to the whole of Europe. Terrorists are too weak to accomplish their goals by force of arms. They are sometimes strong enough, however, to persuade audiences to do as they want by altering the audience's beliefs about certain matters such as the terrorist's ability to impose costs and their degree of commitment to their cause.

The most recent wave of terrorism is global in its scope and is linked to violent religious extremism. It has evolved out of complex causes. These include the globalization, cultural, social and political crises, and the alienation of young people living in foreign societies. For terrorist organisations, the best place to establish themselves are the so called failed states where the government is not functioning in a way that it secures the basic principles and conditions for a sovereign state. In such states, it is easier to acquire some territories and persuade people to fight for some common goal, as the civil war is already on, they just need to choose sides. For this reason, Europe has to give an alternative way for the local residents that happen to live in a state which is in a war regime.[46]

---

[46] https://www.consilium.europa.eu/uedocs/cmsUpload/78367.pdf

Refugee crisis

The Regional conflict in the Middle East is the main reason why so many refugees are trying to get into Europe. These people appreciate our values of democracy, freedom of speech and religion. It would be a complete failure to disallow entrance for them, because in such a way we would admit to be in a state of war against Islam which is totally against our fundamental values where we, the Europeans, emphasize the freedom of religion. According to the previously mentioned strategy of terrorist organisations with the objective to scare and divide societies that would start to question the decisions made by their local governments or international organisations, Europe must develop internal institutions which are responsible for allowing entrance to refugees and a huge impact would be the establishment of a horizontal legislative initiative to oblige Member States to share information. Here is a quote from Guy Verhofstadt: "As long as we do not create a European Intelligence System, as long as we don't have 'mandatory sharing', the loopholes will continue. It will still be possible for a terrorist as Abdeslam, who was stopped and questioned in Cambrai the night of the Paris attacks, to continue on his way because the French police didn't know him.

However, the Belgian police knew him very well, but the information was not shared."[47]

Proliferation of Weapons of Mass Destruction

Proliferation of Weapons of Mass Destruction is potentially the greatest threat to our security and many of us do not pay enough attention to this problem. As international organisations have gradually drafted a coherent international treaty regime and attacked the issue of export controls, the spread of WMD have decreased. Nevertheless, taking into account the situation in the Middle East, Europe is now entering a new and dangerous period that raises the possibility of a WMD arms race. The development in the area of the biological sciences may increase the potency of biological weapons in the coming years; threats regarding attacks with chemical and radiological materials are also a serious possibility.

Organized Crime

Europe is a prime target for organized crime. Such criminal activities are often linked to weak or failing states. Profiting from such activities as selling drugs have fueled the weakening of state structures in

---

[47] http://www.alde.eu/nc/press/press-and-release-news/press-release/article/schengen-finished-without-european-border-and-coast-guard-guy-verhofstadt-46488/

several drug-producing countries. All these activities undermine both the rule of law and social order itself which are core values for European society. In addition, it destroys many people lives and does not allow European society to develop and thrive.

Russia

The biggest threat in the geopolitical area for European Union certainly is Russia. Their actions in Crimea and Middle East have shown that a huge difference remains on how the Western and Eastern society see the world and what their main values are. What amazes the author the most is the fact how the Kremlin denied the obvious violations of the United Nations charter which prohibits any interference of other sovereign state territorial integrity even though there was clear evidence that the Russian military equipment and soldiers have supported the rebels fighting against the Ukrainian army. [48] [49] Considering these actions, Europe should condemn Russian military interference and stand strong against the possible cancellation of economic sanctions against Russia. Furthermore, a coherent and active cooperation with NATO is

---

[48] http://www.un.org/en/sections/un-charter/chapter-i/index.html

[49] http://www.atlanticcouncil.org/en/publications/reports/hiding-in-plain-sight-putin-s-war-in-ukraine-and-boris-nemtsov-s-putin-war

required in order to strengthen the outside borders of the European Union, especially in the Eastern Europe.

To sum up, there are more than enough problems to solve and the rising tensions between NATO and Russia only adds fuel to fire in the international relations. Yet, Europe has to deal with the refugee crisis where we should look at the picture from a wider perspective- what will happen to those innocent people who are seeking peaceful life and life in a democratic society if we would turn our backs against them?

How will the situation develop if Europe does not respond to the terrorist attacks in Paris and allow the "Daesh" to violate the International law in the Middle East region. Will it weaken or strengthen the security risks of terrorism in the world and Europe? Moreover, the strong lobbying from Russia and the economic interests for particular countries should be set aside when lifting of sanctions or the "Nord Stream 2" is discussed. Europe will be successful if it remains united and stand for its core values no matter what.

WILLIAM MOTSMANS
The Multi-Speed Approach - A Solution to Europe's Defence Quagmire?

Since its inception shortly after the Second World War, the project of European unification has had the pursuit of peace at its core. Yet, in the words of the Roman author Vegetius: *si vis pacem, para bellum*. Peace within a (super)nation's borders is hard to maintain if the nation is weak in its defence against external threats.

While accumulated defence spending by European member states is certainly not negligible, even in these financially strained times, their defence capabilities are proportionally low and lack coordination. The result could be observed in recent war games conducted by the RAND Corporation, which concluded that a Russian strike force could reach the outskirts of Riga and Tallinn within 60 hours, leaving both NATO and EU few options in dealing with such a (hypothetical) aggression on its sovereign lands.

This realization should leave readers uncomfortable in light of actual security threats on the European continent and the Mediterranean region. The Ukrainian Revolution of 2014 and consequent war in the Donbass region, the Crimean annexation by the Russian Federation (in spite of a United Nations resolution in opposition) and the attack on Malaysia

Airlines Flight 17 in that same year brought armed conflict close to the borders of the Union for the first time in fifteen years, since the conclusion of the Kosovo war in 1999. The Syrian Civil War, which began in 2011, and the rise of Islamic State have given occasion to a multilateral conflict which affects numerous countries and factions both in the region and overseas and which has inspired several attacks against civilian targets on the sovereign soil of EU member states. Participation of Russian armed forces have provided key insights into recent technological advances and their concrete strategic and tactical implementation, demonstrating a more than adequate capability to go toe to toe with NATO forces.

In light of these recent events; of chronic underspending on defence capabilities by several NATO member states relative to budgetary guidelines, as illustrated in the figure below; and of the increased threat of attacks by foreign actors on EU soil, it is time for the member states of the European Union to re-evaluate their defence policies and, more specifically, to establish a deeper joint commitment.

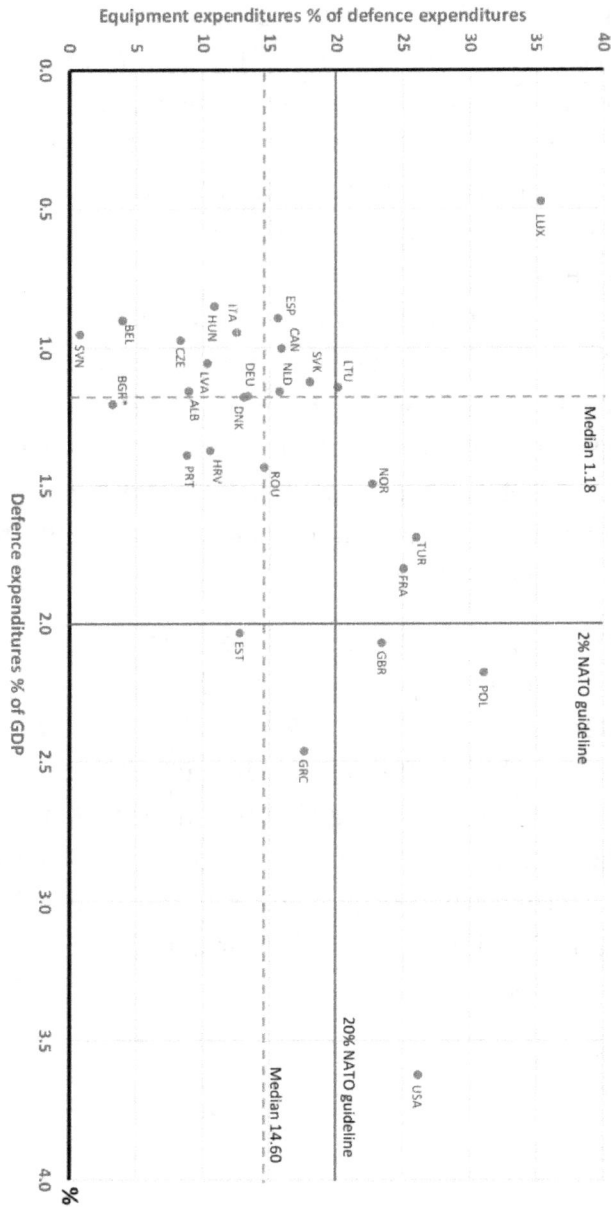

Since time immemorable, defence is a core responsibility of the government. Even in libertarian circles, most criticism concerning defence policy is aimed at overspending, mandatory conscription and other limitations of personal and economic freedom, rather than at the concept of a state-supported military force capable of defending national borders in itself.

However, defence is historically a policy area that is confined to the authority of sovereign nation states. Alliances can be and have been forged in a trade-off between sovereignty and security, yet the free-rider problem is more than prevalent in intra-alliance discussions on military spending, as mentioned above, and disagreements regarding optimal composition of armed forces often go a long time without a consensual solution. Commitments to deeper integration are typically impeded by a reflex towards conservation of national sovereignty, especially where intervention abroad is concerned, on the one hand and by nationalistic pride, pertaining to both armed forces and the defence industry, on the other.

A tighter coordination of defence policies between European member states would however offer a number of benefits that are hard to deny, even by the most staunch nationalist: (1) clout on the stage of international politics and diplomacy is often proportional to (a) a (supra)state's size and (b) a military capacity that can be used in tandem with shared political goals; (2) economies of scale enable more advantageous procurement of military equipment; (3) a larger military force, both in terms of manpower and equipment budget, provides more opportunities for specialization, leading to a more versatile defensive arsenal. To some extent, the advent of a shared European foreign policy has led to an initial convergence in the defence area.

Article 42 of the Treaty on European Union provides a legal basis for the establishment of a common security and defence policy, which has been expanded upon by Protocol No 10 on Permanent Structured Cooperation in the Treaty on the Functioning of the European Union. These enable the development of civilian and military capabilities necessary for the realization of a common Union defence policy, a goal which was introduced to the shared political realm of the Union by the Lisbon Treaty in 2007. Their application so far has led to some success, the most visible of which was probably Operation Atalanta by EUNAVFOR off the coast of Somalia.

Additionally, the European Defence Agency, established in 2004, guides and facilitates intra-European cooperation in military capability development, and coordinates several research projects in the defence area. However, its current capacity to effectively impact member states' defence goals remains a point of debate.

Building a political consensus to further integrate European military forces, while necessary, will require ample amounts of both time and political courage; yet maintaining the status quo is hardly an option in view of new challenges to European security.

Therefore, I would propose to fully embrace the options provided by the Permanent Structured Cooperation mechanism, in order to enable systematic coordination of military investment and specialization by distinct groups of member states who specifically share a reciprocal trust relationship, as a result of political, historic and cultural factors, enabling a partial transfer of sovereignty to a multinational level.

This would effectively lead to a differentiated integration into Common Defence Areas within the Union that can pave the way for a deeper, EU-wide security and defence integration, and its less extensive reach facilitates a political consensus: for instance, it would be far easier to convince the Belgian government to coordinate its defence investments with the Dutch, or the Estonian, Lithuanian and Latvian governments to coordinate theirs, than to convince Lithuanian voters of relying for its defence on armed forces shared with the Spanish or the Greek.

The proposed model would provide initial economies of scale necessary to enable investment in maintaining and upgrading military hardware; it would allow member states' armed forces to attain a greater degree of specialization, as they would no longer have to accomplish every possible strategic task (air defence, naval defence, ...) on their own; and it provides an impetus to open up the internal market for the defence industry and to reduce state support to national armaments factories, which to this day remain flagships of national pride, more often than not to the detriment of economic efficiency.

Human and monetary resources released through this streamlining process can be allocated to modernizing the capabilities of member states, in particular where defence against hybrid warfare and cyberwarfare are concerned.

I believe this solution to be an elegant one, that can gain the necessary political traction in a relatively short time, and would lead to a more secure, safe and defendable European Union.

References:

ALDE Roadmap Towards EU Integrated Military Forces

http://www.rand.org/pubs/research_reports/RR125 3.html

http://www.iss.europa.eu/uploads/media/Report_16
.pdf

http://www.gmfus.org/publications/common-
ground-european-defence

http://www.nato.int/cps/en/natohq/news_127537.h
tm

MANEL MSALMI
Towards Cybersecurity: Cyberspace from Fiction to a Real Threat

Reading books like "Neuromancer" makes one feel as if he reads George Orwell's 1984, a fictional book with illusionary characters and far from being real. However, history demonstrated that these books can be a reading of the future. The word "cyberspace" which was coined by William Gibson in his novel "Burning chrome" written in 1982 in which he depicts the story of two freelance hackers (Wikipedia) and introduces the idea of cybercrime by penetrating into security systems demonstrates that we are living in an era in which cybercrime is one of the threats to our individual rights and freedoms.

In "Neuromancer", we witness a legitimization of violating other people's cyberspace. A term defined by Gibson as "a consensual hallucination experienced daily by billions of legitimate operators". Cyberspace which is a common space which allows millions of people around the world to have access to information and share knowledge can be a target to multiple violations especially personal data such as credit cards and online shopping.

Another risk that any internet user can undergo according to Edward Snowden is mass surveillance which can go beyond commercial concerns to reach the private sphere. This would raise the debate concerning privacy and freedom and to what extent can we trust internet and is the government allowed to have access to personal data and under which circumstances?

The revelations advocated by Edward Snowden regarding mass surveillance and America's National Security Agency(NSA) leaves us lost between different views and expectations and torn between two different choices security versus democracy and freedom "For some, like Congresswoman Zoe Lofgren, it is a vitally important issue, one of the biggest of our time: nothing less than the defence of democracy in the digital age"(The Guardian).

Having access to social media accounts such as Facebook, twitter etc. could help identify the profile of an individual and have information about his family, friends and personal relationships. The NSA aims to fight against terrorism which Snowden finds legitimate but he thinks that there are certain limits to online encryption.

EU response

EU lawmakers and member states on Monday 7th 2015 made a deal which "will require online firms such as Google and Amazon, to report serious breaches or face sanctions" (EuroActiv.com). This deal shows that

European governments give much importance to privacy and security and want to fight against cyberattacks by protecting European citizens legally and financially.

This law obliges companies in some specific sectors to follow certain directives aiming at protecting the consumer against hacking and information trafficking. Member states made an agreement to cooperate on cybersecurity which would lead to more coordination for a better security situation in Europe.

Liberal leaders approved this agreement and found that it is the first step towards a single digital European market. Luxembourg's Prime Minister Xavier Bettel who led the negotiation said that it "is an important step towards a more coordinated approach in cybersecurity across Europe". Antana Guoaga MEP (ALDE) said that it is an "important step" towards the security of the information system. (EuroActiv.com)

The need to have a "harmonized approach" as Guoga explained aims to facilitate business services in the European continent by applying the same set of rules to the same companies instead of applying "28 different approaches". The liberal approach hopes to develop a single European market which manages to have cybersecurity and be attractive to investors as well as competitive globally.

Cyberspace and companies

Cyberspace becomes a field for cyber warriors who can be recruited by some countries to do the spy job which raises the issue of cybersecurity and how can we protect data and people facing cybercrime and espionage. In addition, terrorist groups can attack governments, companies and communication networks. "Cyberterrorism is the act of Internet terrorism in terrorist activities, including acts of deliberate, large-scale disruption of computer networks, especially of personal computers attached to the Internet, by the means of tools such as computer viruses." (Wikipedia).

Nonetheless, a cyberattack cannot only be a digital violation, it can also be physically violent and dangerous which was the case in Germany in 2014 with the incident of the still mill or the pipeline explosion in Turkey. Such incidents demonstrate to what extent cyberattacks can be physically harmful and might have severe consequences especially when it has to do with nuclear energy or oil which was the case in Saudi Arabia in 2012.

European companies and government agencies can be a victim of some hackers who hope to steal financial data. In order to fight against cybercrime and espionage, there should be an organisation between the different branches of the same company in Europe for instance by encouraging the internet Service providers (ISP's) policy for instance and sharing intelligence about risks with each other. (The Economist, Defending the Digital Frontier).

The Data protection Reform adopted in Brussels on December 21st 2015 aims at " strengthening the citizens' fundamental rights in the digital age and facilitate business by simplifying rules for companies in the Digital Single Market" (European Commission, communiqué de presse).This reform guarantees both the rights of the European citizen such as freedom of speech, freedom of expression etc. and the "one stop shop" policy, a policy which helps European companies to deal with one single market.

Moreover, this reform guaranties the individual rights by having control on their personal data which will be beneficial for individuals and businesses. SME's as well will benefit from a measure which aims at stimulating economic growth, facilitating data processing activities and save money. Thanks to the Data Protection Reform, SME's will not need to consult local lawyers because the "data protection law will be the same in 14 European countries"

Certainly, Europe faces nowadays a huge security challenge starting by the terrorist threat and the use of internet in cybercrime as well as hacking and espionage. Cybersecurity is essential to ensure a healthy online economy and secure prosperity. European member states need, however, to launch a Digital Single Market strategy as well as to ensure the consumer's rights and confidence. By adopting the Data Protection Reform and the EU cybersecurity law agreement, Europe made a huge step toward a balance between guaranteeing the citizens' rights and freedom as well as fighting against cybercrime.

References:

http://europa.eu/rapid/press-release_MEMO-15-6385_en.htm

https://isiseurope.wordpress.com/2014/06/19/the-need-for-greater-transatlantic-cybersecurity-cooperation/

http://www.tripwire.com/state-of-security/security-data-protection/security-controls/cyberterrorists-attack-on-critical-infrastructure-could-be-imminent/

http://www.theguardian.com/world/interactive/2013/nov/01/snowden-nsa-files-surveillance-revelations-decoded#section/

https://en.wikipedia.org/wiki/Neuromancer

MARCUS NILSEN
Is the European Union's Mutual Assistance Clause 42.7 a Failure?

This text was first presented at a conference in Brussels four days prior to the terrorist attacks in Brussels. Therefore, the events are not included in this paper. It is worth noting that no parts of the EU's defence were activated as a result of the attack in Brussels.

In 2015, the first activation of the parts within the European Union, that aim to protect its members from an external threat, the activation was as a result of the terrorist attack in Paris. It was France that demanded assistance using clause 42.7. The question is whether the clause had real impact and if these safety measures were necessary, and if there might be other solutions to ensure the security of the union.

The terrorist attack in Paris

On the 13th of November 2015, Paris was the target of a comprehensive terrorist attack. The deed was carried out by Daesh and consisted of coordinated bombings across the city, as well as the shooting of hostages. As a result of this gruesome attack, 130 people were killed and 368 were injured. Such an extensive terrorist attack has not been carried out within the EU since the 2004 Madrid bombings[50].

As a reaction to the attack, France announced three months of state of emergency, which allowed the police to conduct house searches without legal review and to put a ban on public demonstrations. Also, the most extensive police operation in the history of the country was launched.[51]

With the Paris terrorist attack came a crisis that reached far beyond the borders of France. This time, the attack from Daesh was a declaration of war against the whole western world. During the EU defence minister meeting in Brussels on the 17th of November, France informed through defence minister Jean-Yves Le Drian, that France was at war and demanded the invocation of clause 42.7 in the EU treaty.[52]

The 42.7 clause in the EU treaty

The EU's mutual assistance clause 42.7 (also known as the EU's mutual defence clause) in the Treaty on European Union (TEU) is the sharpest formulated part of the EU treaty when it comes to EU's defence. It is

---

[50] BBC News

[51] The Guardian

[52] Briefing on the 42.7 clause in the TEU from EPRS, page 5

clear and entrenched that all member states have a duty to fulfil in case of an aggression against a member state. All members are obliged to help the target member state "by all the means in their power". Clause 42.7 in the TEU is usually confused with article 222 in the Treaty on the Functioning of the EU (TFEU), also known as the "solidarity clause". Although there are big similarities between the two, there are critical differences, which are addressed later in this paper.[53]

The mutual assistance clause 42.7 was included in the EU framework through the Lisbon Treaty in 2009. This is the further development of the ideas that have existed since the Union was founded; collaboration to establish peace.

It was during the failed drafting of the Constitutional Treaty, that the question arose if the European Union should have a mutual defence clause similar to NATOs article 5. The driving force for this was France and Germany.

A comprehensive discussion of these issues was conducted in the member countries. But like the Constitutional Treaty itself negotiations failed and neither were adopted. However, when work started to

---

[53] Briefing on the 42.7 clause in the TEU from EPRS, page 2

create what today constitutes the Lisbon Treaty, such a clause was included and later adopted.[54]

The first proposal was more or less a copy of NATO's Article 5. However, it was quickly realised that there were contradictions and shortcomings in the proposal. The idea was to incorporate more than NATO's Article 5 and wanted to interweave the new clause with article 222.

Furthermore, the question was asked what to do with the countries that consider themselves militarily neutral and those that were already members of NATO. The compromise that was reached is also the same as the adopted clause.

This means that those who consider themselves to be militarily neutral (Sweden, Finland, Ireland and Austria) cannot be forced to participate in military operations if an invoking of clause 42.7 is issued. This broadens the options for the assisting country to choose by which means they can actually assist with. With the current text, aid in itself is more the goal then necessarily what the aid consists of.

The same special treatment applies to countries that are both connected to the EU and NATO. These

---

[54] Briefing on the 42.7 clause in the TEU from EPRS, page 2

countries are protected in a way that NATO's Article 5 always are superior to the clause 42.7. In other words: commitments to the EU is secondary to those of NATO. This allows that, if Article 5 is activated, these member states have the right to ignore the invoking of 42.7 clause.[55]

The mutual assistance clause 42.7 say the following:

"7. If a Member State is the victim of armed aggression on its territory, the other Member States shall have towards it an obligation of aid and assistance by all the means in their power, in accordance with Article 51 of the United Nations Charter. This shall not prejudice the specific character of the security and defence policy of certain Member States.

Commitments and cooperation in this area shall be consistent with commitments under the North Atlantic Treaty Organisation, which, for those States which are members of it, remains the foundation of their collective defence and the forum for its implementation."[56]

---

[55] Briefing on the 42.7 clause in the TEU from EPRS, page 3

[56] Treaty on European Union

The difference between Article 222 in the TFEU and the clause 42.7 in the TEU

The solidarity article 222 say the following in its opening paragraph

"1. The Union and its Member States shall act jointly in a spirit of solidarity if a Member State is the object of a terrorist attack or the victim of a natural or man-made disaster. The Union shall mobilise all the instruments at its disposal, including the military resources made available by the Member States"[57]

The difference between clause 42.7 and Article 222 is mainly their extent and focus. Article 222 is designed to take care of events which is not war according to the UN definition. This means terrorism and other events that may occur, for example natural disasters or nuclear accidents. This article is more complicated since it has two different levels within itself and since it is within the EU administration and jurisdiction, unlike the 42.7 clause, which is bilateral. Among other things, this means that the EU could get involved more directly in the process and that the EU court has jurisdiction regarding the activation of Article 222 but not regarding Clause 42.7.[58]

---

[57] Treaty on the Functioning of the EU

[58] Briefing on the 42.7 clause in the TEU from EPRS, page 6

The difference is also in the language. The word solidarity, which also gave the article its nickname, is not found in clause 42.7. This can be seen as merely a linguistic choice, but it is important when discussing the spirit of what the various sections mean. In a measurement of strength between these two, it is clause 42.7 that is the stronger one. This by being more direct and simpler designed by excluding the EU administration.

This is also one of the reasons why France chose to activate the clause 42.7 and not Article 222. It was explained by the French Defence Minister Jean-Yves Le Drian, that France's actions mainly were a 'political act' that the French hope to see translated into 'collaboration capability for French intervention in Syria and Iraq, either by embossing to or support of France in other operations.'[59]

One should also underline that Article 222 has never been activated and therefore like clause 42.7 was untested at the time of the attack.

Has the 42.7 clause worked in reality?

In a resolution in the European Parliament on January 21, 2016, it is stated that the parliament has observed a unanimous support among the member states

---

[59] Briefing on the 42.7 clause in the TEU from EPRS, page 7

towards France activation of clause 42.7. The European Parliament welcomes the response from the member states and that the members are prepared to fully contribute with the support and assistance required. The conclusion is consistent with what clause 42.7 requires from the individual countries. However, it is not clear what has actually been done. When reading the resolution, it is obvious that the parliament is unsatisfied with the outcome. They want to clarify and make additions concerning the protection of the EU.[60]

Perhaps it is not surprising that adjustments and clarifications are necessary when a clause of this nature only has been used once. It can be viewed as a stress test. Furthermore, it is clear that different countries and political groups have and have had different perceptions as to how these rules should be interpreted and applied.

The resolution also raised the question about NATO, emphasizing the importance of NATO and the EU to continue to strengthen their collaboration, and to a greater extent work to synchronize and coordinate their defence and security policy. The European Parliament also highlighted that NATO has a special role in the security and defence of Europe and the

---

[60] European Parliament resolution on January 21, 2016

Atlantic. The parliament emphasizes, above all, that this also applies when it comes to terrorism.[61]

A review of the actual commitments shows that they vary between the member states. It is also difficult to assess the willingness of the member states to help France when no specific requests for assistance are public. The same applies when it comes to the actual operations, depending on the country, the degree of transparency varies. But one can say that the relief effort differs between countries. That is partly explained by the fact that the member states have different capacities and that some countries have their own internal difficulties which must be dealt with.

Some of the bilateral initiatives that have been confirmed come from the UK, Germany, Belgium, Italy and Sweden. The UK has offered France the use of its Akrotiri airbase in Cyprus for the French air force. The British parliament has also provided backing for the airstrikes in Syria.

The German parliament has already approved a German involvement in Syria to fight Daesh. Germany does not rule out an escalation of their involvement if necessary. Germany is also increasing its mission in Mali to relieve the French troops so that they can be relocated, as does Belgium, which had the intention to

---

[61] European Parliament resolution on January 21, 2016

withdraw from Mali, but now will stay indefinitely. Italy has ruled out direct participation in combat in Libya, but it has offered the use of their air bases for the coalition utilization and strengthened its presence in Lebanon. Sweden is one of the countries that consider themselves militarily neutral, and has offered non-military aid directly in Syria. Sweden has also reinforced their support to the Iraqi army, by assisting with the training of troops, as well as extended the mission in Mali.[62]

It is obvious that France has received assistance, but what impact the 42.7 clause actually has had is extremely unclear. France had certainly received assistance without it. This would also have been the case in a situation where France would have refrained from invoking Article 222 or NATOs article 5. However, the main question is whether the EU member countries have met the point of "aid and assistance by all the Means In Their power" as is stated in the 42.7 clause. This is at present time impossible to determine, but only the hesitation about the efficiency and fulfilment of the clause 42.7 is in itself a threat to the European cooperation.[63]

---

[62] Briefing on the 42.7 clause in the TEU from EPRS, page 6

[63] Treaty on European Union, 42.7 clause

Has the 42.7 clause been a failure then?

It is impossible to assess how crucial this clause has been to the efforts that have been made, and it is therefore difficult to determine if it is a failure or not. It is the lack of clarity that the European Parliament in its resolution want to fix and revise, but one must also ask whether this is the right path or if there are better ways to protect Europe.[64]

The parliament has already expressed that NATO has a heavy and special role in protecting Europe. It also says that we must integrate ourselves more with NATO. This is perhaps a strategy to get NATO to become a natural part of the EU, so that the defence of the EU can be fully operated by NATO. Regardless of whether this is currently a hidden agenda or not, it should in the future become an official agenda for the European Union. Why should we try to create rules that still will be secondary to those that some of the member states have towards NATO? This only creates a fragile foundation of the Union to stand on. This problematic issue must be brought up. The effect of this is a differentiated membership in the Union with the current rules. The countries that are members of NATO and those who consider themselves militarily neutral ar given a special treatment that we do not need in the

---

[64] European Parliament resolution on January 21, 2016

Union. It creates a basis for conflict and division in Europe. It is this type of special treatment that is the real threat to the Union. An external threat we can handle, that is what our countries are made to handle. But we are not built for a situation where distrust within the EU is growing strong.[65]

We should look at what we have built between our European countries and consider whether it is worth sacrificing this over trying to resemble NATO. We have a community which today makes it natural for member states to help each other. We should entrust all bilateral defence commitment to NATO and instead urge all EU member states to join NATO.

Conclusion of the current situation

The existing rules for the security and solidarity within the EU is a good idea and has roots back to the Union's founding. But today, we must dare to realise that the EU cannot do everything, and that they also should not. We must dare to raise the issue if the defence of EU territory is best defended with vague and unclear rules, or if it is not better to leave that to NATO. Our union can continue to work with research and coordination in the military field, but we should not pursue a purely defensive collaboration within the framework of the EU. It would be unwise to be careless

---

[65] European Parliament resolution on January 21, 2016

with the wonderful Union that we currently have. Instead, we should be careful and stay away from what has not yet been tried, and instead urge all EU members to join NATO. In the end, it does not matter how our countries are protected. All that matters is that it is actually done.

References:

http://www.bbc.com/news/world-europe-34818994 (18-02-2016)

http://www.theguardian.com/world/2015/nov/16/france-nationwide-state-of-emergency (18-02-2016)

Treaty on European Union

Treaty on the Functioning of the EU

Briefing on the 42.7 clause in the TEU from EPRS, *The EU's mutual assistance clause First ever activation of Article 42(7) TEU.* European Parliamentary Research Service

European Parliament resolution on January 21, 2016 *European Parliament resolution of 21 January 2016 on the mutual defence clause (Article 42(7) TEU) (2015/3034(RSP))*

FILIP RAMBOUSEK
European Defence Cooperation

The current geopolitical situation is less stable than at any point since the end of the Cold War and continues to deteriorate. Russia has openly declared expansionist ambitions, and duly acted on them- something unimaginable even during the Cold War. At the same time, the Middle East and North Africa are in a state of unprecedented instability, signified by but not limited to, ISIS.

Western leaders deserve much of the blame. In their attitude to Russia, they demonstrated a staggering amount of short-sightedness. Much to Eastern Europeans' chagrin, Obama dismissed Governor Romney's 2012 statement that Russia was the USA's foremost geopolitical threat, retorting that "the 1980s are now calling to ask for their foreign policy back".[66]

Today, the debate over the future of European defence policy is absolutely crucial to the European Union itself. As von Clausewitz famously observed, war is the continuation of policy by other means. The lack of ability to make war means a lack of any real foreign policy. A foreign policy cannot exist without a core of

---

[66]http://www.salon.com/2012/10/23/obama_the_80s_called_they _want_their_foreign_policy_back/

deterrence and proof that diplomacy can be backed with coercion. 'Diplomacy without arms is like music without instruments', said Frederik the Great. Similarly, the Union cannot exist as a political union at all if it renounces rights to foreign policy, because the two are inextricably linked. It is impossible to demarcate which legislation only affects the domestic affairs of a state, and thus counts as internal, and where it reaches abroad. Such a state would not possess any political legitimacy to begin with. Therefore, if we aim for an EU as a political, rather than economic union, a Defence Union is necessary.

To some, however, there is little reason or incentive for a change of the current, NATO-centric model. Most EU Member States, after all, are in NATO, the 'strongest alliance that's ever been built', according to former Supreme Allied Commander General Wesley Clark.[67] It has a proven record of deterrence, provides US military backing, and overall credibility. Indeed, the current feeling of complacency in Europe is largely an indicator of how successful NATO has been in providing one of Europe's most peaceful and stable periods of its history.

The argument of this essay, however, is that the deepening of a European Defence Union is in NATO's

---

[67] http://www.bbc.com/news/world-europe-31503859

interest. For many economic and practical reasons, the continuation of the current status quo is not desirable. The fragmentation of forces means that despite massive investments, EU armies are reaping little benefits. This negatively affects their ability to act as a reliable NATO ally, and thus overall NATO capabilities. By outlining economic, as well as operational inefficiencies of the current status quo, this essay will argue that a method of regional cooperation is the best way of deepening EU Defence Union integration, and thus strengthening NATO.

Economic Inefficiency

Despite America's "Pacific Pivot", the US continues to bail out Europe's defence, and will probably continue to do so even after the 2016 election. As a result, there is little motivation for EU states to increase their defence spending. Aside from Bernie Sanders, who hardly mentions foreign policy,[68] and Donald Trump, a wildcard in all aspects of policy, the establishment candidates remain committed to America's long standing commitment to NATO. Clinton, generally considered more interventionist 'more naturally

---

[68] https://www.yahoo.com/politics/how-president-bernie-sanders-would-handle-foreign-127259111076.html

adapted' to geopolitics than Obama.[69] The same is true on the Republican spectrum; candidates such as Kasich or Rubio would serve 'far more as commander in chief than as diplomat in chief, wielding the great American military hammer to address problems that bear very little resemblance to a nail'.[70] In short, American commitment to NATO is not in danger, and Europe is therefore likely to rest in relative safety for the foreseeable future.

As a result, individual EU member states have generally seen an uncompromising trend of decreasing defence spending. This is a result of the post-Cold War era of complacency, as well as the financial crisis.

The resulting momentum has been so powerful, that even with the rise of ISIS and Russian aggression, only the Baltic states, Poland, the Netherlands, and Romania have increased the % of their GDP spent on defence, with five others- the UK, Italy, Hungary, Bulgaria, and Germany- actually decreasing their defence budget.[71]

---

[69] http://foreignpolicy.com/2015/11/06/hillary-clinton-doctrine-obama-interventionist-tough-minded-president/

[70] http://foreignpolicy.com/2015/11/06/hillary-clinton-doctrine-obama-interventionist-tough-minded-president/

[71] http://www.wsj.com/articles/nato-calls-for-rise-in-defence-spending-by-alliance-members-1434978193

Importantly, the "Big Three"- the UK, Germany and France- are either lowering or, in the case of France, flat lining their defence budgets.[72]

This all is despite the 2014 Wales Pledge, in which NATO states reaffirmed their NATO commitments:[73]

Allies currently meeting the NATO guideline to spend a minimum of 2% of their Gross Domestic Product (GDP) on defence will aim to continue to do so... Allies whose current proportion of GDP spent on defence is below this level will:

- *Halt any decline in defence expenditure;*
- *Aim to increase defence expenditure in real terms as GDP grows;*

It is crucial to keep in mind that NATO members were not shaken into action even by the Russian invasion of Ukraine and annexation of Crimea. While NATO itself may be acutely aware of its shortcomings, its members are simply unwilling to accept the risks associated with the new geopolitical situation.

It is therefore clear that on the national level, Member States simply lack the political will to reform their budgets and take national defence responsibly. At the same time, NATO has proven incapable- both legally

---

[72]http:/www.europeanleadershipnetwork.org/medialibrary/2015/0 2/20/04389e1d/ELN%20NATO%20Budgets%20Brief.pdf

[73]http://www.nato.int/cps/en/natohq/official_texts_112964.htm

and politically- to persuade their members to honor their commitments to mutual defence. Indeed, the European Leadership Network's defence study concludes that 'pressure from NATO allies has had little effect on the big European defence spenders':[74]

Nevertheless, coming so soon after the Wales Declaration, the figures presented in this document do not reflect NATO's rhetoric about events in Ukraine being a 'game-changer' for European security... several countries are clearly continuing with business as usual, apparently without taking into account the Wales Summit decisions, or – in some cases - doing the exact opposite of what the Alliance as a whole pledged to do in September 2014

The money that does get spent is then more often than not spent efficiently. 'Take Belgium', says Professor Alexander Matelaar of the Free University of Brussels (VUB):[75]

At present, nearly three-quarters of the budget goes on personnel spending [with] 24-25% going on operating costs for current operations and training. But that leaves... at present less than 1% for signing new contracts for purchasing new kit, and modernising the equipment. And of course on

---

[74]http:/www.europeanleadershipnetwork.org/medialibrary/2015/0 2/20/04389e1d/ELN%20NATO%20Budgets%20Brief.pdf

[75] http://www.bbc.com/news/world-europe-31503859

that basis, you can keep things afloat for a short period, but it's an absolute killer over the longer haul.

It is obvious that the current status quo of European defence is severely marred by its inefficiencies.
On the EU level, however, the picture is altogether different. Combined, EU member states currently spend €190 billion on defence.[76] That makes the EU the world's second biggest spender, behind the US but ahead of China. In 2015, the US spent around €500 billion on defence related matters.[77] While the gap between US and EU defence spending remains large, the EU's budget still provides it with a potential for a modern and effective fighting force.

Operational Inefficiency

In fact, on the EU level, these investments allow for a collective armed force of 1.5 million troops- nearly as

---

[76] http://www.bloombergview.com/articles/2015-03-12/the-eu-and-whose-army-

[77]

http://www.telegraph.co.uk/news/uknews/defence/11936179/What-are-the-biggest-defence-budgets-in-the-world.html many as the US, and twice as many as Russia, for instance.[78]

However, despite massive investments and huge armed forces, the EU remains an incapable military force. At a recent Defence Union workshop hosted by the European Parliament, with representatives from the European Defence Agency, NATO and the EEAS, among other institutions, the experts agreed that despite size of the budget and personnel numbers, the EU's fighting effectivity only stands between 10-15% that of the United States. Similar estimates have been made by other observers.[79] In other words, while the US only spends two and a half times as much as the EU, it reaps ten times the benefits of the EU. The main problem in EU defence are not financial resources, but rather the efficiency with which they are used.

As a result, military capabilities of EU states are limited. When it comes to the military powerhouses of

---

[78] http://www.bloombergview.com/articles/2015-03-12/the-eu-and-whose-army-

[79]

https://www.washingtonpost.com/news/worldviews/wp/2015/02/19/germanys-army-is-so-under-equipped-that-it-used-broomsticks-instead-of-machine-guns/

Europe (France, the UK, and Germany), the picture is bleak. Out of this "Big Three",[80]

the United Kingdom is the only one with a fully capable fighting force. It is also the only country whose higher tactical and operational commands possess combat experience. French capabilities are limited, and more so Germany's, who is also in these terms limited politically.

Capabilities have sunk to alarming levels. The United Kingdom, a long-standing naval superpower, has been forced to ask NATO for assistance in patrolling its own waters. Britain called upon NATO sea patrol planes in order to track a Russian submarine off the coast of Scotland in November 2014.[81] Similarly, Germany has been running into complications when attempting to carry out its anti-piracy commitments off the Horn of Africa due to a lack of mission-ready equipment.[82] In 2014, The Washington Post obtained leaked

---

[80]http://www.cevroinstitut.cz/upload/ck/files/PCTR/Publikace/2015/policy%20paper%20Czech%20Republic%20in%C2%A0CSDP%20of%C2%A0the%C2%A0EU%20(web).pdf

[81]

http://www.telegraph.co.uk/news/uknews/defence/11283926/Britain-forced-to-ask-Nato-to-track-Russian-submarine-in-Scottish-waters.html

[82] http://www.theguardian.com/world/2014/oct/07/germany-military-hardware-disrepair-exposure

documents which 'detailed the shocking state of disrepair of Germany's military hardware':[83]

Only one of its four submarines is operational. Only 70 of its 180 GTK Boxer armoured vehicles are fit for deployment. Just seven of the German Navy's fleet of 43 helicopters are flightworthy.

The most famous case of acute shortages of equipment in the German army came in 2015, when, at a NATO exercise, it had to resort to installing painted broomsticks on their fighting vehicles instead of heavy machine guns.[84]

In conclusion, it is obvious that despite possessing massive, well-funded armed forces on the theoretical, EU level, individual Member States are by and large militarily completely incapable. The exceptions may be the UK, Germany, and France, whose recent Mali operations demonstrated its ability to carry out small scale operations. However, as we saw, even these

---

[83] https://www.washingtonpost.com/world/europe/the-german-military-faces-a-major-challenge-from-disrepair/2014/09/30/e0b7997c-ea40-42be-a68b-e1d45a87b926_story.html

[84]

https://www.washingtonpost.com/news/worldviews/wp/2015/02/19/germanys-army-is-so-under-equipped-that-it-used-broomsticks-instead-of-machine-guns/

European military superpowers are in fact severely underfunded and lack the necessary equipment to fulfil their NATO commitments, or even national defence.

The Way Forward

As we saw, EU Member States possess much greater potential as a unified military unit than on their own.

The difficult question revolves around what this new Defence Union would look like, and how it could be put together. Two general "schools of thought" have been proposed on this matter. Last year, Jean-Claude Juncker called for 'a common army among the Europeans'.[85] Former NATO Secretary General and chief EU diplomat Javier Solana criticised this idea, saying that 'having a flag behind which this army appears' is not a realistic approach; instead, he suggested,[86]

we have to put together the integrated capabilities of different countries but not create an army in the sense of a national army... We are talking about a union, which is like the monetary union, the energy union or the digital union.

---

[85] http://www.theguardian.com/world/2015/mar/08/jean-claude-juncker-calls-for-eu-army-european-commission-miltary

[86] http://www.euractiv.com/section/security/interview/solana-a-wake-up-call-for-a-european-defence-union/

Something that is putting in common what we have, integrated much more and acts in a much more coordinated fashion. This is what we have in mind.

The "Juncker plan", i.e. the outright creation of an EU army, is currently impossible. According to NATO's Allied Command Transformation's representative in Europe, Vice-Admiral Ignacio Horcada, argues that the establishment of a new EU army would currently simply be too expensive.[87] The other side of the coin is the absence of political will, especially in the UK. The UK government's reaction to Juncker's proposal was clear and expected: 'our position is crystal clear that defence is a national – not an EU – responsibility and that there is no prospect of that position changing and no prospect of a European army', said a government spokesman.[88] Among other things, the UK voices legitimate concerns over the willingness of an EU army to defend the Falkland Islands, or its role in a potential dispute with Spain over Gibraltar. Without the UK, it is difficult to envisage a meaningful EU army.

The aim needs to be firmly set on goals which are achievable in the short term. Some may be more symbolic, such as the elevation of the EU Parliament's

---

[87] Interview with author.

[88] http://www.theguardian.com/world/2015/mar/08/jean-claude-juncker-calls-for-eu-army-european-commission-miltary

Security and Defence Subcommittee to a full committee level. The creation of an EU Commissioner for Defence would carry more practical implications, and signify a dedication to the deepening of interoperability and resource pooling.

In the medium to long term, the path that the EU should choose is more closely related to the "Solana plan", focusing stead on deepening interoperability and, crucially, regional cooperation. An example of this is the cooperation of Belgium, the Netherlands, and Luxembourg (BENELUX).

Indeed, the BENELUX agreement has met a good degree of success. Initially, the Netherlands and Belgium began formally cooperating in naval defence matters in 1996. "Benesam", as this naval cooperative agreement is known, provides the two countries 'with an integrated command, common training and maintenance facilities for frigates and mine hunters'.[89]

More recently, the two countries, along with Luxembourg, 'agreed to share surveillance and protection of their air spaces', including the authorisation to shoot down renegade aircraft in each

---

[89]http://www.clingendael.nl/sites/default/files/The%20Future%20o f%20the%20Benelux%20Defence%20Cooperation.pdf

other's territory.[90] Starting in 2017, the plan is also to include cooperation in and sharing of training facilities. The agreement is unprecedented in its depth of cooperation: overall, these include 'logistic and maintenance; education and training; executing military tasks, procurement of equipment.'[91] It is also ground-breaking 'because it is the first time countries agree that a foreign air force may operate and potentially shoot down a civilian plane over its territory.'[92]

As is the case in virtually all other EU countries, this degree of cooperation was driven by the need to increase the countries' value for money, with the common aim being 'increasing military efficiency by bringing our forces together, sharing costs where possible and increasing the output of our operational capacities.'[93]

So far, regional cluster military cooperation has been a success. According to the Dutch Ministry of Defence,

---

[90] https://euobserver.com/news/127885

[91]http://www.clingendael.nl/sites/default/files/The%20Future%20of%20the%20Benelux%20Defence%20Cooperation.pdf

[92] https://euobserver.com/news/127885

[93]http://www.clingendael.nl/sites/default/files/The%20Future%20of%20the%20Benelux%20Defence%20Cooperation.pdf

both sides 'view their cooperation as a win-win situation and it constitutes a textbook example of European bi-national cooperation.'[94] Crucially, the issue of national sovereignty-a matter of utmost sensitivity to most European politicians- has been resolved with relative ease:[95]

Benesam is already showing for more than a decade that capabilities can be kept by sharing sovereignty. Common facilities for education and training, for logistics and maintenance do not encroach upon national sovereignty in decision-making on deployments. Thus, the Benesam model is regarded by the Benelux countries as a proven case for deeper cooperation in other areas. It could equally serve as an example for other clusters.

Indeed, this seems to be the best model and way forward for the integration of Member States' armed forces. Firstly, countries are much more at ease when cooperating in sensitive military matters with neighboring states, with whom they are likely to closely share common culture and history. This is

---

[94] https://www.defensie.nl/english/topics/international-cooperation/contents/other-countries/the-belgian-and-netherlands-navies-under-1-command

[95] http://www.clingendael.nl/sites/default/files/The%20Future%20of%20the%20Benelux%20Defence%20Cooperation.pdf

emphasized due to the current distrust between "old" and "new" Europe.

Secondly, there is plenty of potential for this method, given the amount of already existing regional clusters, such as the Visegrad 4, Nordic Defence Cooperation, or the Baltic Defence Cooperation. [96]

Thirdly, this method is a natural and gradual way of increasing interoperability and cooperation. Eventually, we should envisage an EU of a good degree of interoperability overall, but with an extremely high degree within these regional clusters. Once this has been achieved, the EU can move on to increasing cooperation between these clusters themselves. This will be easier because a degree of trust will have been gained in joining forces with other countries, and because there will simply be fewer cooperative bonds to build.

Moreover, these regional clusters will be able to exploit their specializations, which is partly required by NATO membership, and exploit their national identity and culture. As we saw in the This is already happening on the national level. Countries with limited resources, such as the Czech Republic, no longer aim to be able to deploy a multifaceted force capable of defending its

---

[96] "ALDE roadmap towards EU Integrated Military Forces".

territory. Instead, it has aimed to specialize on a small number of fields, in this case battlefield medicine and CBRN (Chemical, biological, radiological and nuclear) defence in which it can provide added value to its allies.

Lastly, it appears that there is no actual alternative to this model. We simply cannot aim for outright amalgamation of all EU armed forces, as explained above. The opposition from key members, especially the United Kingdom, is much too real for such a gargantuan task.

While such regional cooperation will focus on the above described tasks such as logistics, training and procurement, Member States should also complement their cluster cooperation with a standing, deployable battle group. In fact, on Polish initiative, the Visegrad Battlegroup should become a 'flagship'[97] permanent formation, further deepening 'systemic and systematic defence planning, exercises and perhaps even procurement and maintenance'.[98]According to Vice Admiral Horcada, these should be multi-national units permanently stationed on the Alliance's Eastern Flank. This will as well as significantly increase deterrence, as

---

[97] http://visegradrevue.eu/visegrad-battlegroup-a-flagship-that-should-not-substitute-for-real-defence-cooperation/

[98] http://spectator.sme.sk/c/20051913/polish-passion-for-visegrad.html

an attack on a multi-national unit is much more likely to elicit the concerned states honouring of their commitment to the mutual defence cause.

NATO and the Defence Union

Many opponents of the European Defence Union argue that creating a parallel, competing defence force alongside NATO would only weaken our collective security. 'If our nations faced a serious security threat, who would we want to rely on – NATO or the EU? The question answers itself', says Geoffrey Van Orden, Conservative's spokesman on defence and security.[99]

The argument of this essay, however, is that the deepening of a European Defence Union is in fact in NATO's interest. As we saw above, NATO states have decreased their capabilities to such an extreme extent that they are virtually unable to operate. A Defence Union, composed for now of various regional clusters, would increase NATO's ability to act and increase its specialization.

We should also keep in mind that the role of NATO has- and still is- undergoing some dramatic changes. Indeed, it may be that Article 5 itself, the cornerstone

---

[99] http://www.theguardian.com/world/2015/mar/08/jean-claude-juncker-calls-for-eu-army-european-commission-miltary

of collective security, may need revision. For instance:[100]

How do you decide what constitutes an attack when the nature of warfare has changed: no longer state on state warfare, but little green men - Russian special forces in unmarked military uniform - crossing the border, and supporting separatists...the single most important purpose of this Russian hybrid warfare [is] to try to circumvent the activation of NATO's Article 5.'

This is all the more important in a world where the line between external defence and internal security has become rather blurry. Foreign aggressive entities, like ISIS and Russia, do not attack by sending armed columns against our borders; instead, they employ terrorism as well as disinformation, cyber-attacks and various other methods, respectively.

Given shared European borders and financial markets, EU states are currently adopting a shared plethora of security risks, but aim to defend itself isolated from one another. This is an altogether implausible scenario.

Conclusion

This essay aimed to show that an EU Defence Union is inextricably linked to the EU with political ambitions.

---

[100] http://www.bbc.com/news/world-europe-31503859

As the EU has transformed itself from a common market into a political union, the continuing failure of EU leaders to produce a common defence policy is tantamount to a failure of the entire political project.

Despite certain scaremongers, such a Defence Union is in NATO's interest, and will increase the security of the Western world. As we saw, individual EU NATO Member States lack the political will to fulfil their NATO obligations, and many of them have now become virtually incapable of carrying out their defence requirements. Similarly, NATO has failed in attempting to persuade its Members to remain responsible and valuable allies.

While the outright creation of an EU army is currently impossible, as well as inadvisable, this essay outlined feasible steps of regional cooperation within already existing schemes, which have proven to function. At the same time, these regional clusters should aim to permanently maintain at least one EU Battlegroup each.

ALEKO STOYANOV
The Russian Military Challenge to the EU in the Context of the Ukraine Crisis

The Ukraine crisis raised a question whether a new, although more limited regional war, could emerge in Eastern Europe. Some of Russia's neighbours – the three Baltic States and Poland, who had been occupied by Russia in the past, have expressed such concerns. The numerous breaches of the airspace and territorial waters of those countries (and other EU member states) by Russian military airplanes and vessels as well as Moscow's militaristic rhetoric have corroborated those fears.

Nonetheless, despite these worrisome signals Russia is lacking both the ambition and the capacity to implement such plans. Regardless of the modernisation in recent years, the Russian army still falls behind the (combined) military strength of the EU and it is rather a shadow of the former soviet army.

After the collapse of the USSR, the Russian army lost considerable amount of its strength. From 5 million troops in 1991 the army shrank to around 1.2 million personnel a decade later.[101]

---

[101]Matthew Aid, Today's Russian Army Is a Shadow of the Former Soviet Army of the Cold War, 30 September 2014,

The obsolete equipment, poor leadership, understaffing and mismanagement have weakened the Russian army. The two wars in Chechnya only underpinned this perception and made the contrast with NATO's technology-advanced armed forces more apparent.

Even in 2008, when Russia achieved a swiftly and decisive victory over Georgia, the operation suffered from plethora of shortcomings – poor tactical and operational planning, difficult coordination between different army groups, unmanned regiments, cases of "friendly fire", etc.[102]

Hence, the Georgian war became a turning point for Russia which launched a deep and comprehensive military reform later in 2008. It aimed to secure three main objectives – improving the organisation by restructuring of the armed forces into a mainly professional volunteer army and replacing the divisions with smaller but easily deployable brigades[103]; optimising the number of personnel to 1 million people and rearming the Russian army with

---

http://www.matthewaid.com/post/98797449611/todays-russian-army-is-a-shadow-of-the-former

[102] Gustav Gressel, Russia's Quiet Military Revolution, and What It Means for Europe, European Council on Foreign Relations, p. 2
[103] One division consists of around 13 000 troops while a brigade comprises some 4000 troops

new and modern weapons,[104] including 2300 tanks, 1200 helicopters and planes, 50 surface ships and 28 submarines, 100 satellites.[105] In order to achieve these ambitious goals the Russian government increased significantly its military budget, from $61 billion in 2008 to $70 billion in 2011 to reach the ever high (since the collapse of the USSR) of $91 billion in 2014[106] which made Russia the biggest arm spender in Europe. For example, in 2014 the UK has allocated $60 billion, France $62 billion, Germany $46 billion and Italy $31 billion for their defences.[107]Moreover, as a share of its GDP Russia spends more for its defence – 4.5% than the US and China, whose military budgets represent 3.5% and 2.06% of their GDP's, respectively.[108]

The results of the reorganisation of the Russian army and the increased expenditure have become visible during the occupation of Crimea. Within less than a

---

[104] Jonas Grätz, Russia's Military Reform: Progress and Hurdles, CSS Analyses in Security Policy , No. 152, April 2014, ETH Zürich, p. 2

[105] Nikolas K. Gvosdev, The Bear Awakens: Russia's Military is Back, National Interest, 12 November 2014, http://www.nationalinterest.org/commentary/russias-military-back-9181

[106] Retrieved from Stockholm International Peace Research Institute Military Expenditure Database: http://www.sipri.org/research/armaments/milex/milex database/milex database

[107] Ibid

[108] Ibid

month in an impressive, prompt, well-coordinated and almost bloodless campaign[109] the Russian Special Forces managed to put under control the whole peninsula, an achievement that surprised many military experts. Moreover, during the campaign in Eastern Ukraine Russia maintained between 40 000 and 150 000 men in full combat readiness across the border with Ukraine, as simultaneously Moscow conducted manoeuvres in other part of Russia comprising up to 80 000 troops of all arms which exceeds even the number of Russian armed forces involved in the second Chechen war.[110]

The occupation of Crimea, the support for the rebels in Eastern Ukraine as well as the recent Russian military intervention in Syria signify for the transformation of the Russian armed forces. Nonetheless, along with the progress in some spheres, mainly in the structure and reorganisation of the Russian army there are still significant problems in terms of personnel and rearmament that probably will not be resolved by 2020 when the military reform is scheduled to be completed.

---

[109] John Simpson, Russia's Crimea Plan Detailed, Secret and Successful, BBC, Europe, 19 March 2014, http://www.bbc.com/news/world-europe-26644082
[110] Gustav Gressel, Russia's Quiet Military Revolution, and What It Means for Europe, European Council on Foreign Relations, p. 4

As mentioned earlier the plan envisages the Russian army to reach 1 million professional soldiers. The figure of the actual size of the Russian armed forces varies. According to some estimations the Russian army in 2014 comprised around 700 000 servicemen and women,[111] while a more recent study suggests that this number has risen to 771 000.[112]

However, from them less than the half - 295 000 are contract soldiers[113] and the Russian General Staff aim is to increase their number to 425 000 by January 2017[114] which might be a difficult task. A significant part of the hired troops leave after the three-year contract expires as in 2013, 35 000 have done so.[115]Further problems are caused by lack of motivation, health problems and alcohol abuse among the contract soldiers.[116] In addition, Russia's

[111] Jonas Grätz, Russia's Military Reform: Progress and Hurdles, CSS Analyses in Security Policy , N0. 152, April 2014, ETH Zürich, p. 2
[112] Elisabeth Braw, Russia's Conscription Conundrum, Foreign Affairs, 25 August 2015,
https://www.foreignaffairs.com/articles/russia-fsu/2015-08-25/russias-conscription-conundrum
[113] Pavel Baev, Ukraine: A Test for Russian Military Reform, Russie Nei Reports No. 19, May 2015, p. 23
[114] Elisabeth Braw, Russia's Conscription Conundrum, Foreign Affairs, 25 August 2015,
https://www.foreignaffairs.com/articles/russia-fsu/2015-08-25/russias-conscription-conundrum
[115] Jonas Grätz, Russia's Military Reform: Progress and Hurdles, CSS Analyses in Security Policy , No. 152, April 2014, ETH Zürich, p. 3
[116] Ibid

downward demographic trend continues. It is expected that the number of 18-years old men in Russia will drop from 1.1 million in 2007 to 630 000 in 2017, as only two-thirds of them will be fit for military service.[117]

The rearmament process of the Russian army does not go smoothly either. There has been a delay in supply of new weapons. It is planned that by 2020 70% of the Russian troops will be equipped with modern weapons (no older than 10 years) and by the spring of 2014 only 19% have met that objective.[118]

Moreover, the military procurement which relies chiefly on the Russian domestic defence industry complex suffers from plethora of drawbacks. The Russian factories are lacking innovations and their staff and production facilities are outdated, which combined with central planning relicts and corruption cause late delivery problems.[119] For instance, in 2013 only 15% to 20% of all procurement projects, planned for the first half of that year were completed on time.[120]

---

[117] Margarete Klein and Kristian Pester, Russia's Armed Forces on Modernisation Course, SWP Comments, Stiftung Wissenschaft und Politik, January 2014, p. 4

[118] Jonas Grätz, Russia's Military Reform: Progress and Hurdles, CSS Analyses in Security Policy , No. 152, April 2014, ETH Zürich, p. 3

[119] Margarete Klein and Kristian Pester, Russia's Armed Forces on Modernisation Course, SWP Comments, Stiftung Wissenschaft und Politik, January 2014, p. 4

[120] Ibid

In order to close the knowhow gap and expertise in the production of certain arms Russia made purchases of Mistral-type helicopter carriers from France and armoured vehicles from Italy.[121] However, due to EU's economic sanctions those shipments are currently frozen and at present Russia faces great difficulties to supply its military complex with the needed materials and technologies which affects the speed of its rearmament programme. In addition, the devaluation of the rubble makes the whole process much more expensive which will cut the number of produced arms - tanks, missiles, corvettes and aircrafts by a half.[122]

Despite Moscow's intention to allocate 4% of its GDP to defence in 2016[123] the EU economic sanctions combined with the low energy prices will probably continue to affect negatively the Russian economy. In this scenario, Russia might be unable to continue the modernization of its army with the desired pace as

---

[121] Ibid p. 5

[122] Matthew Bodner, Anna Dolgov, Putin Warns Russian Defence Industry Not to Fall Behind, Moscow Times, 19 July 2015, http://www.themoscowtimes.com/business/article/putin-warns-russian-defence-industry-not-to-fall-behind/525853.html

[123] Matthew Bodner, Russian Military Spending to Increase by Less Than 1% Next Year, Moscow Times, 26 October 2015, http://www.themoscowtimes.com/news/article/russian-military-spending-to-increase-by-less-than-1-next-year/540362.html

even the solid currency reserves on which the Kremlin relied so far have started to deplete.[124]

At last but not least, the plans of the Russian government to use the spending in its military complex as a (at least partial) remedy for the economic troubles by creating more jobs and boost the GDP would have a short-term effect that, however would come at the expense of a long-term fiscal stability.[125]

The EU, on the other hand, does not have a single unitary army. Nonetheless, in terms of number of troops, financial resources and technological capacity the EU surpasses Russia significantly. According to the European Defence Agency (EDA) in 2013 the EU has spent €186 billion ($205 billion) which is more than twice of what Russia has earmarked in 2014 as the number of EU military personnel equalled to 1 436 000 people.[126] The EU's naval and air forces are also superior to that of Russia.[127] However, despite its

---

[124] Holly Ellyatt, Russia's Reserve Fund Could Run Empty In 2016, CNBC, 27 October 2015, http://www.cnbc.com/2015/10/27/russias-reserve-fund-could-run-empty-in-2016.html

[125] Richard Connolly, Troubled Times: Stagnation, Sanctions and the Prospects for Economic Reform in Russia, Research Paper, Chatham House, February 2015, p. 16

[126] European Defence Agency, Defence Data Portal, https://www.eda.europa.eu/info-hub/defence-data-portal/EDA/year/2013#1

[127] Gustav Gressel, Russia's Quiet Military Revolution, and What It Means for Europe, European Council on Foreign Relations, p. 7

military advantage the EU has also some weak spots. In first place, in the past two decades the EU armed forces have been involved mainly in peace keeping operations and assisting in natural disasters which has weakened their combat capabilities. Furthermore, the little or no military exercises and low deployable readiness (the EDA has rated the EU forces only 30.9% combat-ready while for Russia this percentage reaches 65%)[128] raise the question of the actual strength of the EU armies.

Moreover, unlike Russia who is a unitary actor, the EU does not have a centralised European military command which could mobilise a common European army to fight a foreign aggressor. Hence, in case of an armed conflict this would give an advantage to Russia which would be able to take swifter decisions and deploy faster its troops to the battlefield.

A further, but not a lesser issue is the willingness of the Europeans to fight. Against the backdrop of a growing tensions with Moscow the main military powers in Europe have either cut or frozen their military spending in 2015 as none of them would reach the agreed threshold of 2% of national's GDP agreed at NATO's Wales Summit in December 2014.[129] In

---

[128] Ibid, p. 8

[129] Denitsa Raynova and Ian Kearns, Report: Six European Members of NATO Will Cut Defence Spending and Break Agreement Made at

addition, the report by Pew Research Centre, announced last year, revealed that less than the half of the respondents in the six biggest EU countries (all of which are NATO members) think their governments should engage in military actions against Russia in case the latter gets into "a serious military conflict" with one of its NATO neighbours.[130] For instance, in Italy this percentage was 40%, in France 47%, in Germany 38%, in the UK 49% and in both Poland and Spain 48%.[131] These trends hide also a serious risk to undermine NATO's credibility which derives from Article 5 of the North Atlantic Treaty where:

"The Parties agree that an armed attack against one or more of them...shall be considered an attack against them all and... each of them... will assist the Party or Parties so attacked by taking...action as it deems necessary, including the use of armed force..."[132]

Nonetheless, Article 5 allows for a broad interpretation of what these necessary actions might be. It provides

---

Wales Summit, Atlantic Council, 26 February 2015, http://www.atlanticcouncil.org/blogs/natosource/report-six-european-members-of-nato-will-cut-defence-spending-and-break-agreement-made-in-wales

[130] Bridget Kendall, Poll Finds Nato's Europeans Wary of Russia Confrontation, BBC, Europe, 10 June 2015, http://www.bbc.com/news/world-europe-33072093

[131] Ibid

[132] Official Text of The North Atlantic Treaty, NATO, http://www.nato.int/cps/en/natohq/official_texts_17120.htm

for use of force but it does not make it mandatory or automatically. Moreover, having in mind that NATO's principal decision-making body - the North-Atlantic Council (NAC) takes decision by unanimity,[133]a decision for a possible military response in case of Russian attack against, for instance, any of the Baltic States could be obstructed by one or several countries who might not perceive the threat as grave as the affected country. In addition, in the context of the "hybrid warfare" (which blends conventional/unconventional, regular/irregular, and information and cyber warfare[134]) that Russia applied in Ukraine, it might become more difficult for NATO states to reach an agreement whether such actions could be classified as an "armed attack" or not.

Alternatively to NATO's Article 5, the EU could resort to Article 42/7 of the Lisbon Treaty, which guarantees the security of the member states.[135] In this way the treaty could provide also for EU members who are not part of NATO - Finland and Sweden and who are faced with increased number of airspaces breaches by

---

[133] The North Atlantic Council, NATO, 11 November 2014, http://www.nato.int/cps/en/natolive/topics_49763.htm

[134] Damien Van Puyvelde, Hybrid War – Does It Even Exist?, NATO Review Magazine, http://www.nato.int/docu/Review/2015/Also-in-2015/hybrid-modern-future-warfare-russia-ukraine/EN/index.htm

[135] Gustav Gressel, Russia's Quiet Military Revolution, and What It Means for Europe, European Council on Foreign Relations, p. 15

Russian military.[136] So far this article has not been applied broadly[137] but it gives another option in case NATO is unable to reach unanimity.[138]

In sum, despite its recent modernization the Russian armed forces are still falling behind in terms of personnel and military equipment. The Russian army might be unmatched in Eastern Europe but its capacity is limited. It would be hard to imagine that currently Russia would be able to build a 600 000 army to invade the Baltic States as the USSR once did.[139] Nonetheless, Moscow demonstrated that it is eager and willing to use military force in order to secure its objectives, a sign that should be neither neglected nor exaggerated by the EU. The EU member states would need to show a real commitment to its security by enhancing its military capabilities, improving coordination and cooperation, investing in defence and participating in joint military trainings. By doing so the EU will send a

---

[136] Charles Duxbury and Christina Zander, Sweden Complains to Russia Over Airspace Violation, The Wall Street Journal, 19 September 2014, http://www.wsj.com/articles/sweden-complains-to-russia-over-airspace-violation-1411163347

[137] After the Paris terrorist attacks in November last year, France was the first EU country to resort to article 42/7 of the Lisbon Treaty. However, it remains to be seen how effective its application would be in practice.

[138] Gustav Gressel, Russia's Quiet Military Revolution, and What It Means for Europe, ECFR, p. 15

[139] Pavel Baev, Ukraine: A Test for Russian Military Reform, Russie Nei Reports No. 19, May 2015, p. 26

strong signal to the Kremlin that it will defend the values, principles and norms that it stands for.

References:

Bridget Kendall, Poll Finds NATO's Europeans Wary of Russia Confrontation, BBC, Europe, 10 June 2015, http://www.bbc.com/news/world-europe-33072093.

Charles Duxbury and Christina Zander, Sweden Complains to Russia Over Airspace Violation, The Wall Street Journal, 19 September 2014, http://www.wsj.com/articles/sweden-complains-to-russia-over-airspace-violation-1411163347.

Damien Van Puyvelde, Hybrid War – Does It Even Exist?, NATO Review Magazine, http://www.nato.int/docu/Review/2015/Also-in-2015/hybrid-modern-future-warfare-russia-ukraine/EN/index.htm.

Denitsa Raynova and Ian Kearns, Report: Six European Members of NATO Will Cut Defence Spending and Break Agreement Made at Wales Summit, Atlantic Council, 26 February 2015, http://www.atlanticcouncil.org/blogs/natosource/report-six-european-members-of-nato-will-cut-defence-spending-and-break-agreement-made-in-wales.

Elisabeth Braw, Russia's Conscription Conundrum, Foreign Affairs, 25 August 2015, https://www.foreignaffairs.com/articles/russia-fsu/2015-08-25/russias-conscription-conundrum.

European Defence Agency, Defence Data Portal, https://www.eda.europa.eu/info-hub/defence-data-portal/EDA/year/2013#1.

Gustav Gressel, Russia's Quiet Military Revolution, and What It Means for Europe, European Council on Foreign Relations, p. 2.

Holly Ellyatt, Russia's Reserve Fund Could Run Empty In 2016, CNBC, 27 October 2015, http://www.cnbc.com/2015/10/27/russias-reserve-fund-could-run-empty-in-2016.html.

John Simpson, Russia's Crimea Plan Detailed, Secret and Successful, BBC, Europe, 19 March 2014, http://www.bbc.com/news/world-europe-26644082.

Jonas Grätz, Russia's Military Reform: Progress and Hurdles, CSS Analyses in Security Policy, N0. 152, April 2014, ETH Zürich, p. 2.

Margarete Klein and Kristian Pester, Russia's Armed Forces on Modernisation Course, SWP Comments, Stiftung Wissenschaft und Politik, January 2014, p. 4.

Matthew Aid, Today's Russian Army Is a Shadow of the Former Soviet Army of the Cold War, 30 September 2014, http://www.matthewaid.com/post/98797449611/todays-russian-army-is-a-shadow-of-the-former.

Matthew Bodner, Anna Dolgov, Putin Warns Russian Defence Industry Not to Fall Behind, Moscow Times, 19 July 2015, http://www.themoscowtimes.com/business/article/putin-warns-russian-defence-industry-not-to-fall-behind/525853.html.

Matthew Bodner, Russian Military Spending to Increase by Less Than 1% Next Year, Moscow Times, 26 October 2015, http://www.themoscowtimes.com/news/article/russian-military-spending-to-increase-by-less-than-1-next-year/540362.html.

Nikolas K. Gvosdev, The Bear Awakens: Russia's Military is Back, National Interest, 12 November 2014, http://www.nationalinterest.org/commentary/russias-military-back-9181.

Official Text of The North Atlantic Treaty, NATO, http://www.nato.int/cps/en/natohq/official_texts_17120.htm.

Pavel Baev, Ukraine: A Test for Russian Military Reform, Russie Nei Reports No. 19, May 2015, p. 23.

Richard Connolly, Troubled Times: Stagnation, Sanctions and the Prospects for Economic Reform in Russia, Research Paper, Chatham House, February 2015, p. 16.

Stockholm International Peace Research Institute Military Expenditure Database: http://www.sipri.org/research/armaments/milex/milex_database/milex_database.

The North Atlantic Council, NATO, 11 November 2014, http://www.nato.int/cps/en/natolive/topics_49763.htm.

FILIP SUPEL
Transnational European Military Forces Supporting NATO

In 1999, the European Council summit in Helsinki, Finland (December 10-11) officially announced the establishment of the European Security and Defence Policy (ESDP). Its objectives have become, first of all, to increase the capacity of the EU to conduct independent operations and decision-making in the event of a crisis. Although these provisions were to become independent of what NATO decides in a particular case, the North Atlantic Alliance remained the basis of the Common defence. It declared an increased cooperation with NATO, to increase the potential of the EU and speed up the reaction to crises.

This was in order to better carry out the "Petersberg Tasks", proclaimed a so-called European Headline Goal. It assumed that by the end of 2003 the creation of a body consisting of 50-60 thousand soldiers, who will be able, within 60 days, to carry out any "Petersberg Tasks" for at least one year. These troops were to include land, sea and air forces. During the realization of the objective, difficulties arose, which made it necessary to extend the target deadline and therefore on 18 June 2004 the old objective was replaced with the new operational objective 2010.

That's the past. Now we have some big dangers in the United Europe: the refugee crisis, the precarious situation in Ukraine and the unpredictable foreign policy of the Russian Federation. But unfortunately, the countries in the European Union can't get the most out of our military potential.

European members of NATO and the EU, though officially supporting the idea of cooperation and aspiration to be global players, still pose the national security against the common interest. It is believed, that international cooperation in the field of defence policy results in the loss of sovereignty by individual nation-states.

Meanwhile, no European country today is strong enough to act alone. Even the two leading military powers of Europe, United Kingdom and France, are no longer in a position to carry out the entire spectrum of military operations. They have to rely on each other, as well as the United States, as they did for example in the case of operations in Libya.

Some European countries with smaller military potential offer narrow specialization instead. They demand, however, that they can decide themselves on the use of the equipment. Meanwhile, the fear of the supposed resignation of sovereignty and mutual suspicion will not strengthen neither the transatlantic ties, nor the position of Europe in the world. Consistent reduction of defence spending could lead to a situation, in which the European defence industry will be marginalized to the extent, that the Old Continent will be forced to import military equipment. Europe will be dependent on foreign suppliers, either from Asia or from the US or Latin America.

Confirmation of how big the military potential of European Union is can be found in figures: the number of EU forces should indicate that out of approx. 4.3 million soldiers serving in the armies of all NATO countries combined, approx. 2 million, i.e. about half, are from EU Member States. (The number of troops throughout the Union, including six countries not belonging to the Alliance, is only minimally larger).

The American armed forces, consisting of more than 1.5 million soldiers, represent approx. 1/3 of the entire capacity of NATO but are at the same time a quarter fewer than the forces of EU member states. Theoretically, the human potential of the European Union (also taking into account a number of reservists and various paramilitary forces) always looks grand. This is evident, as among other world powers only China has a more numerous army (approx. 2.5 million).

But the fundamental issue is the financial expenditure for military purposes, including not only the budgets for the maintenance of the army, but also the purchase of new weapons and research expenses of a military.

The NATO members combined make up approx. 60% of the armaments expenditure of the world, and approx. 40 % of it is by USA alone. In NATO the American preponderance is still more assertive: they finance 60 % of the total expenditure, while the participation of EU Member States amount to only 1/3.

From the data above it is evident, that this potential is indeed significantly lower than for the US, but at the same time, the European Union combined coming in second place after the US on the world scale does look very impressive. Theoretically speaking, this would give the EU a good starting position to try to increase the status of its military power. At the same time, however, it is evident that individual member states lead their own policies in this regard, taking into account first of all their particular national interests.

In my opinion, we should establish transnational European military forces, that would be responsible for supporting NATO forces in ensuring the security in Europe. These forces would support the EU's foreign and security policy as well as serve the integration of the units of each country on the basis of Eurocorps, the creation of which, however, requires closer cooperation of the defence industries and the creation of a uniform strategy and budget. In principle, such units would be subject to EU institutions, but would be complementary to NATO, which would remain the basis for European Union security. Nevertheless, this plan should be addressed to all EU countries, including those which do not belong to the Alliance.

For example, the total value of the military budgets of the EU members is only 45 percent height of that of the Pentagon, and the operational capacity is at the level of 10-15 percent of the capacity of the US Army. Europe must face to the facts. The national armies have weakened, and the EU countries are facing problems which solutions are beyond their capabilities. The idea of a European defence is to rely on the recovery of the ability to act to secure the achievements of European integration.

The creation of a unitary defence policy, "a European army", would be extremely beneficial for my country. Poland certainly would play a significant role in the decision-making structure. A strong position in the Polish part of Euroland would impact not only on opportunities in the context of the acquisition of new technology and defence contractors, but also to increase its importance in all of the NATO structures. Currently, our role in the Pact is very average. Despite the declaration of the allies, especially the US, on the priority of our position as a European ally, concrete evidence of our significance has been absent for many years. For this reason, Polish interest in the development of the idea of a "European army" is most reasonable and justified. In the rapidly changing world, Europe appears old, rich and apathetic to the dynamics and Poland, along with it, is lagging behind.

In the struggle for the support of electorates, European politicians of all ideologies try to live up to an increasingly unrealistic promise of performance – and as a result political visions and realities become increasingly divergent, also in the field of defence. Meanwhile, Americans reoriented their strategic interests to the Pacific a long time ago, leaving Europe on the side-lines, while the Russians consistently implement the Eurasian Union project, which is to strengthen the Russian position as an intermediary between the Western economics and the dynamically developing Asia, providing a stable economic and technological transfer. I hope, that this "world train", in which defence policy and a new organisation of forces play a very important role, did not leave us, Europeans, too far behind.

ANASTASIIA YASYR
New Concepts Regarding Security

During a long period of time, the discussion on new approaches to security has been dominated by multiplicity and complexity, with a special emphasis on three emerging concepts that have been increasingly used in security studies: globalization, human security and securitization. As for me, it is important to give a brief overview of the international security landscape.

Today's picture of the nature of "security" have undergone a process of profound transformation. Perhaps for the first time in history, the military dimension of security has lost its once undisputed pre-eminence. The relative decline of the military component of security is also reflected in the fact that providing security has become a more complex task, which implies the ability to mobilize multiple assets alongside military ones, and which can no longer be entrusted exclusively to the state. In this section, the emphasis is consequently put on the structural trends that challenge the Westphalian way of thinking about international relations and its practice of international security: a mix of alliance politics, collective security, multilateralism and national policies that have been the operational context of transatlantic security relations and of an unbalanced relationship between the United States (US) and European countries for decades.

Therefore, the focus here is on the structural factors that affect the capacity of single states, even the most powerful ones, to exercise leadership in the security domain. This by no means imply that states are powerless or less important than in the past, but only that they are no longer the only game in town. To a large extent, the structural trends highlighted here coexist and interact with traditional international security practices, and states remain, by and large, the key players. But these transformations require new forms of cooperation and leadership. This transformation is best described as a broadening and a deepening of the security agenda.

"Broadening" the security agenda implies the inclusion of non-military threats such as terrorism, as well as security challenges, such as environmental scarcity, pandemics or mass refugee movements. "Deepening" the security agenda means considering referent-objects other than the state, such as individuals, social groups or planet Earth. These two dynamics are interlinked, as addressing non-military threats and challenges often entails moving beyond states as referent-objects. Yet several authors argue that, while broadening the spectrum of threats taken into consideration, security analysis should retain the state as the main referent-object as it remains, ultimately, the crucial actor in addressing these threats. In light of this debate, the present report places the emphasis on the challenges in terms of capacity and leadership posed to states by novel dynamics in international security.

These new structural trends in international security are multiple and multi-dimensional. In the attempt of making sense of them, three conceptual lenses appear particularly useful: globalization, human security and securitization.

Globalization has been the most important feature in transforming the international security landscape. It has increased the interconnectedness between societies and states, led to a contraction of space and time – thus creating global challenges as well as global public goods – and decreased the capacity of any state to manage global security threats and risks alone. More concretely, new technologies and the ease with which people, goods, money and ideas cross national borders have transformed international security in two ways.

Firstly, they have contributed to altering the nature of war, leading to a diminution of inter-state wars and a multiplication of low-intensity conflicts, insurgencies, and ethnic and civil wars (Mackinlay 2014). Secondly, globalization has undermined the capacity of states to address security and military challenges on their own, and has changed the balance between state and non-state actors (Freedman 2002).

Particularly illustrative of the consequences of globalization is the centrality of networks in international security (Slaughter 2012), whether epistemic networks fostering the creation of norms or covered networks engaging in illicit activities, ranging from terrorism to drug and human trafficking and the smuggling of nuclear know-how and materials. In accounting for new challenges, the notion of human security has emerged as one of the most influential attempts at re-conceptualizing security. This approach advocates a people-centred, universalist and non-military focus that takes due account of threats to human life such as underdevelopment, poverty and deprivation.

Among the major conceptual and normative shifts that the concept of human security has brought about are a different view of the state and a questioning of its unsurpassable sovereignty in international security. Human security is premised on the assumption that, for many people around the globe, the state is not so much a security provider as in fact the main threat to the upholding of their basic rights (Miller 2001). The concept of human security has been criticized, however, for its lack of analytical rigor, particularly because it stretches security to such an extent that it becomes conflated with development, health, inequality and overall well-being.

This line of criticism points to a securitization pattern that has affected a growing number of policy areas since the end of the Cold War. "Securitization" refers to the process by which specific problems are constructed as security issues.

More specifically, securitization occurs when a concern is identified and declared as posing an existential threat to a designated referent-object and requiring the adoption of extraordinary or even emergency measures that usually extend the legal prerogatives of the securitizing actor while trumping the freedom of society at large (Buzan, Waver and Wilde 1998).

Analysts of securitization have overall been rather critical of its consequences. Neil MacFarlane and Yuen Foong Khong (2006), among others, have pointed out that re-conceptualizing development in security terms has neither generated an increased flow of resources (financial, human or political), nor led to an overall improvement in critical development problems. Other scholars go further and argue that defining something as a security issue might actually be counter-productive or even dangerous in that it legitimizes the suspension of civil liberties.

References:

Chestnut, Sheena (2007), "Illicit Activity and Proliferation. North Korean Smuggling Networks", International Security, Vol. 32, No. 1 (Summer), p. 80-111.

Kaldor, Mary (2000), New and Old Wars. Organized Violence in a Global Era, Stanford, Stanford University Press.

Mackinlay, John (2014), "Globalisation and Insurgency", Adephi Papers, No. 352 (November).

MacFarlane, S. Neil, and Khong, Yuen Foong (2006), Human Security and the UN. A Critical History, Bloomington, Indiana University Press.

Miller, Benjamin (2001), "The Concept of Security: Should it be Redefined?", The Journal of Strategic Studies, Vol. 24, No. 2 (June), p. 13-42.

The Authors

Hrvoje Bašić is Croatian. He is a member of LYMEC member organisation Mladi hrvatski liberali.

Ganna Bazilo is Ukrainian. She is a member of LYMEC member organisation European Youth of Ukraine.

Friso Bonga is Dutch. He is an individual member of LYMEC.

Laurens Bynens is Belgian. He is an advisor at ELF member organisation Liberaal Kenniscentrum

Katalin Cseh is Hungarian. She is an individual member of LYMEC.

Benjamin Fievet is French. He is an individual member of LYMEC.

Vedrana Gujić is Croatian. She is the former president of LYMEC (2014-16).

Maximilian Heilmann is German. He is a member of LYMEC member organisation Junge Liberale JuLis.

Emma Janson is Swedish. She is an individual member of LYMEC.

Jorge de Jesus is Portuguese. He is an individual member of LYMEC.

Lina Karklina is Latvian. She is a member of LYMEC member organisation Attistibai Youth.

Edgars Lejnieks is Latvian. He is a member of LYMEC member organisation Attistibai Youth.

William Motsmans is Belgian. He is a member of LYMEC member organisation Jong VLD.

Manel Msalmi is Belgian-Tunisian. She is an individual member of ALDE Party.

Marcus Nielsen is Swedish. He is a member of LYMEC member organisation Liberala Ungdomsförbundet.

Aleko Stoyanov is Bulgarian. He is an individual member of LYMEC.

Filip Supel is Polish. He is a member of ALDE Party member Nowoczezna.

Danica Vihinen is Finnish. She is the secretary general of LYMEC.

Anastasia Yasyr is Ukrainian. She is a member of LYMEC member organisation European Youth of Ukraine.

The Publishers

The European Liberal Forum (ELF) is the foundation of the European Liberal Democrats, the ALDE Party. ELF consists of several European think tanks, political foundations and institutes and operates as an umbrella organisation for them. The foundation issues publications on Liberalism and European public policy issues and offers space for the discussion of European politics.

The European Liberal Youth (LYMEC) is a pan-European youth organisation seeking to promote liberal values throughout the EU as the youth organisation of the ALDE Party and its parliamentary group in the European Parliament. LYMEC is made up of Member Organisations and Individual Members and it is active across the breadth and diversity of the European continent. LYMEC's central aim is the creation of a liberal and federal Europe.

www.ingramcontent.com/pod-product-compliance
Lightning Source LLC
Chambersburg PA
CBHW060508290526
45791CB00001B/325